The Afghan Papers

Committing Britain to War in Helmand, 2005–06

Edited by Michael Clarke

www.rusi.org

Royal United Services Institute for Defence and Security Studies

The Afghan Papers: Committing Britain to War in Helmand, 2005–06
Edited by Michael Clarke
First published 2011

Whitehall Papers series

Series Editor: Professor Malcolm Chalmers
Editors: Adrian Johnson and Ashlee Godwin

RUSI is a Registered Charity (No. 210639)
ISBN 978-0-415-52593-0

Published on behalf of the Royal United Services Institute for Defence and Security Studies
by
Routledge Journals, an imprint of Taylor & Francis, 4 Park Square, Milton Park, Abingdon OX14 4RN

SUBSCRIPTIONS
Please send subscription orders to:

USA/Canada: Taylor & Francis Inc., Journals Department, 325 Chestnut Street, 8th Floor, Philadelphia, PA 19106 USA

UK/Rest of World: Routledge Journals, T&F Customer Services, T&F Informa UK Ltd, Sheepen Place, Colchester, Essex, CO3 3LP UK

All rights reserved. No part of this publication may be reprinted or reproduced or utilised in any form or by any electronic, mechanical, or other means, now known or hereafter invented, including photocopying and recording, or in any information storage or retrieval system, without permission in writing from the publisher.

Contents

About the Authors

Nick Beadle

Nick Beadle is a former Private Secretary to successive Secretaries of State for Defence and a cross-Whitehall senior adviser on policy for operations. He led the Cabinet Office Afghanistan/Pakistan Strategy and Communications teams, 2008–10, and served in Baghdad, 2004–05, as the coalition's Senior Adviser to the Iraqi Ministry of Defence. He has also worked in No 10 and the Foreign Office, and on NATO, European Union and UN policy. Most recently he was attached to the National Security Secretariat on the British government's response to the Libya uprising.

Desmond Bowen

Desmond Bowen is a retired senior civil servant, working over the last decade variously in NATO HQ, the Cabinet Office and Ministry of Defence. He retired as the ministry's director general for security policy in 2008. He is now a member of the UN Secretary General's Advisory Board on disarmament matters, a visiting professor at Reading University and the Staff Counsellor for the security and intelligence services.

Professor Michael Clarke

Michael Clarke is currently the Director of the Royal United Services Institute for Defence and Security Studies. Until July 2007, he was the Deputy Vice-Principal and Director of Research Development at King's College London, where he remains a Visiting Professor of Defence Studies. He was the founding Director of the International Policy Institute at King's College London from 2001–05 and Head of the School of Social Science and Public Policy at the university in 2004–05. He was, from 1990 to 2001, the founding Director of the Centre for Defence Studies at King's. He was appointed as Professor of Defence Studies in 1995.

He has been Senior Specialist Adviser to the House of Commons Defence Committee since 1997, having served previously with the House of Commons Foreign Affairs Committee, 1995–97. In 2009 he was appointed to the Prime Minister's National Security Forum in pursuit of the new National Security Strategy, and in 2009 was also appointed to the Chief of the Defence Staff's Strategic Advisory Panel.

General Sir Robert Fry
Sir Robert Fry is chairman of McKinney Rogers, a global business execution consultancy. He is also an adviser to a number of other companies in the banking and security sectors. He is a visiting professor at Reading University, a visiting fellow at Oxford and occasional columnist for the business press. He is a trustee of Help for Heroes and of RUSI. Before business, his military career included posts such as the Commandant General of the Royal Marines, Director of Operations in the MoD and deputy commanding general of coalition forces in Iraq.

Valentina Soria
Valentina Soria is a research analyst at RUSI, where she works in the Counter-Terrorism and Security Programme. She analyses and assesses the terrorist threat to the UK and its potential implications for national security. Her other research work also includes military affairs and defence policy issues. She is a PhD candidate at Reading University; her research focuses on the transformation of Italian and UK defence posture after the end of the Cold War, and looks to explore the importance of differing conceptions of role in shaping national defence policies.

Matthew Willis
Matthew Willis is a Research Associate in the International Security Studies Department at RUSI. NATO's campaign in southern Afghanistan, and in particular the interplay between Alliance and national policies, has been among his longstanding research interests. He is also RUSI's lead researcher on historical, political and commercial trends in the Arctic, with a particular interest in the policies of the coastal states. Matthew completed his Bachelor's degree at the University of Toronto, where his dissertation examined Canadian Arctic foreign policy in a historical perspective. He also studied at the Sorbonne and completed his Master's at the London School of Economics.

Acknowledgements

I am grateful to all those military officers, politicians, defence officials and advisers who have given their time so generously to engage in detailed discussions and to speak to us privately on numerous occasions about the matters covered in this volume, and in some cases for detailed comments on draft papers. Thanks, too, to those who felt able to contribute perspective papers to this collection on what is a sensitive and difficult subject. I am also grateful to Professor Malcolm Chalmers, General Editor of the Whitehall Paper series, for his overall guidance and his detailed and very helpful comments on the material. Great thanks also to Adrian Johnson and Ashlee Godwin in the RUSI Publications department for excellent editing under pressure. I also owe a special gratitude to my research colleague Valentina Soria, who has worked with me throughout this study both as a co-writer and project director and with whom I co-authored the earlier study on this issue in the *RUSI Journal*. My sincere thanks to them all.

Professor Michael Clarke

Acronyms and Abbreviations

ARRC	Allied Rapid Reaction Corps
CDS	Chief of the Defence Staff
CJO	Chief of Joint Operations
COIN	Counter-insurgency
DCDS(C)	Deputy Chief of the Defence Staff (Commitments)
DfID	Department for International Development
DND	Department of National Defence (Canada)
DOC	Director of Operational Capabilities
FRES	Future Rapid Effects System
HCDC	House of Commons Defence Committee
IED	Improvised Explosive Device
ISAF	International Security Assistance Force
KFOR	Kosovo Force
MND	Multinational Division
NATO	North Atlantic Treaty Organization
PCRU	Post-Conflict Reconstruction Unit
PJHQ	Permanent Joint Headquarters
PRT	Provincial Reconstruction Team
QIP	Quick-impact project
RC	Regional Command
RUSI	Royal United Services Institute
SACEUR	Supreme Allied Commander Europe
SFOR	Stabilisation Force
UK	United Kingdom
UOR	Urgent Operational Requirement
US	United States

Maps

Afghanistan: Expansion of ISAF mission by stage, 2001–06.

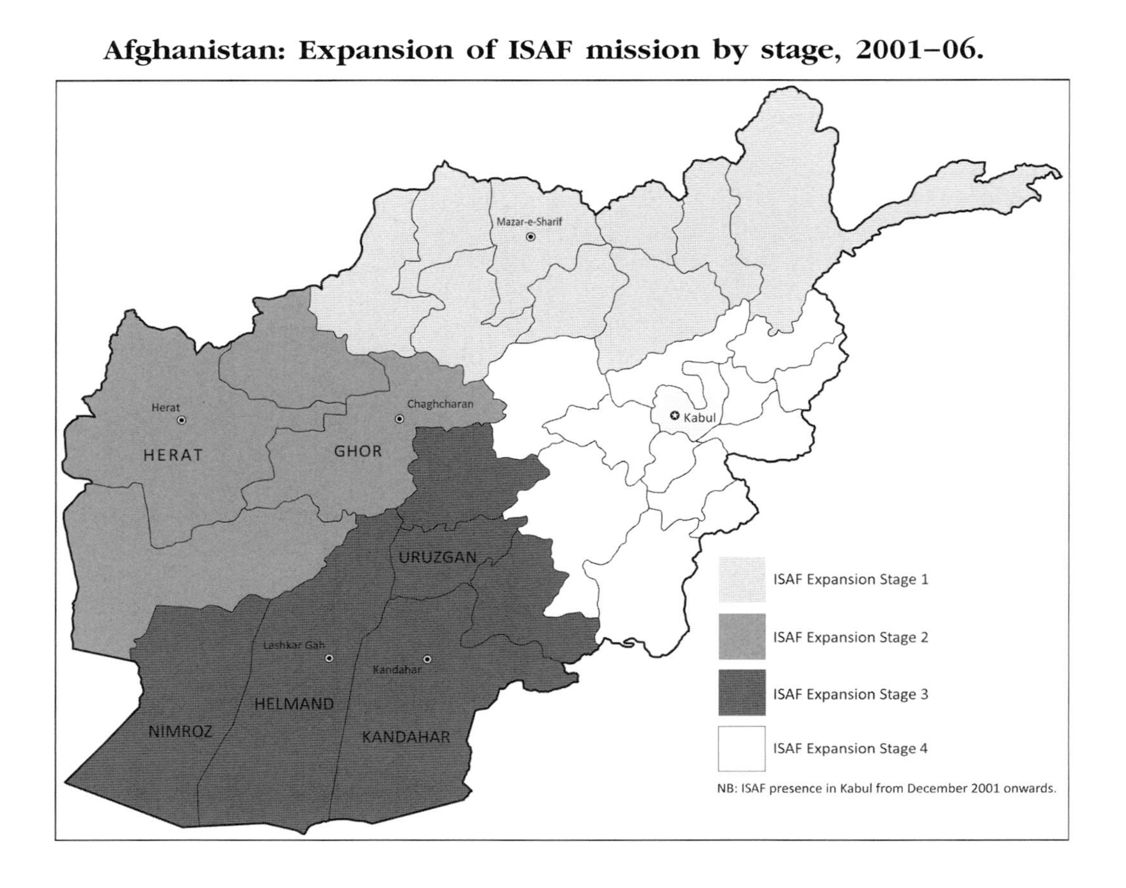

Northern Helmand Province, Afghanistan.

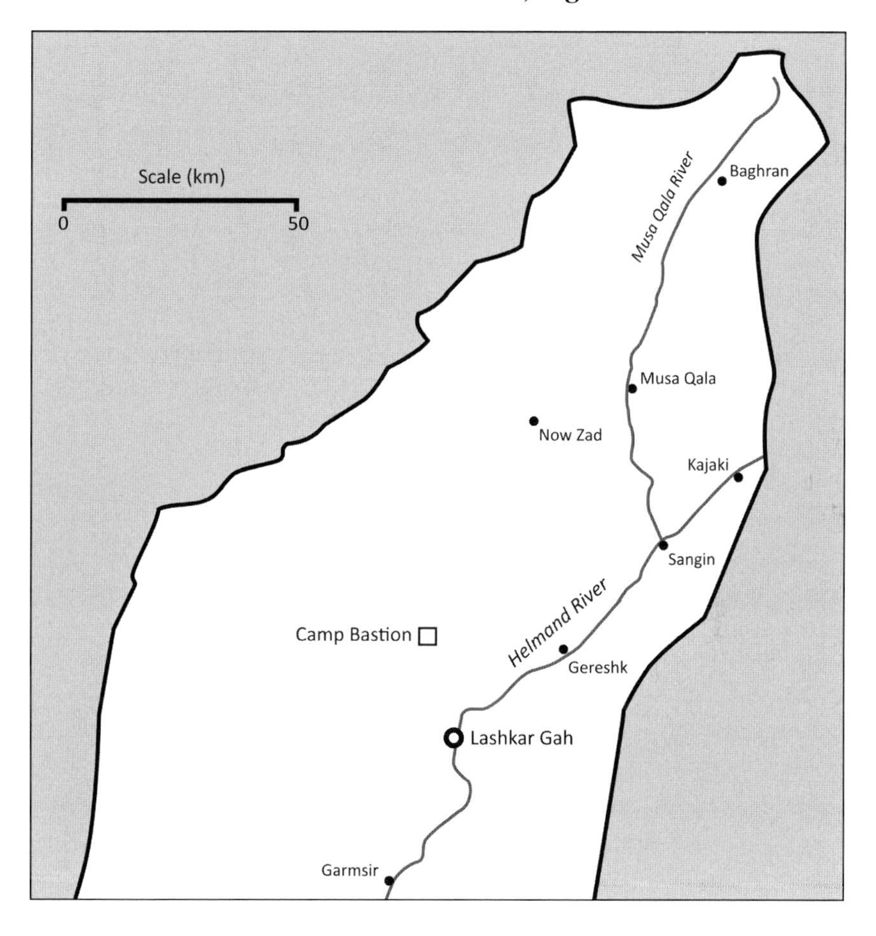

INTRODUCTION

MICHAEL CLARKE

The armed forces of the United Kingdom have now, at the time of writing, been involved in Afghanistan for exactly a decade. By the time the forces draw down from combat roles in 2015, they will have been engaged for almost a decade and a half. Nor will this be the end of the commitment. Some UK forces will remain in a mentoring and support role for the Afghan National Security Forces for some years thereafter. The political commitment to create a sustainable Afghan state and deny international terrorists any ungoverned space in the country remains open-ended.

This represents a long conflict for the UK, undertaken for objectives that remain politically controversial, both nationally and internationally. The British were committed to this Afghan campaign from the very beginning when the Taliban government was ejected from the territory. UK special forces were evident alongside the Northern Alliance in the north of the country around Mazar-e-Sharif during the first campaign against the Taliban and UK troops were engaged from the start in the deployment of the UN-mandated International Security Assistance Force (ISAF) of December 2001. In 2002 more British units were involved in assisting US forces sweeping mountainous areas in the south of the country. For a decade, all three armed services have contributed in a range of roles and on a continuous basis to the Afghanistan campaign.

Nevertheless, it was the deployment of a battlegroup into Helmand in spring 2006 that turned the UK's commitment to Afghanistan from a 'military operation' into a 'war'. The current chief of the Defence Staff, General Sir David Richards, headed NATO's first command of ISAF in 2006. When he returned to the UK, he offered a sober assessment of the prospects facing ISAF forces and in his next post, as Commander-in-Chief (Land), he put the British Army explicitly on a war footing to meet the challenges that Afghanistan posed.[1] Since then, there has been no doubting that the UK has been involved in a small but difficult war in Afghanistan.

How this came about is increasingly controversial. Different answers to the question also play directly into a number of on-going security debates. The Strategic Defence and Security Review of 2010 raised the question of how good the UK is at making strategic decisions. The report of the Ministry of Defence's Defence Reform Unit recommends some important changes in the machinery of defence decision-making. The coalition government elected in 2010 established a National Security Council to improve security strategy throughout Whitehall and more than one parliamentary select committee is scrutinising the way strategic decision-making is handled within the system.[2] The question of whether Britain went sleep-walking into a war that it should have avoided, or whether there are good national interest reasons why it is performing a role in Afghanistan, will be a *leitmotif* of many debates about British strategy and how it is handled in the difficult years to come between now and 2020, when the forces and the strategy are supposed to reach a new 'balance' after all the recent reviews.

For understandable reasons, governments find it difficult to discuss in public the origins and rationales of Britain's military operations while service personnel are still engaged. The Chilcot

---

[1] Ministry of Defence Press Release, 30 October 2009.

[2] HM Government, *Securing Britain in an Age of Uncertainty: The Strategic Defence and Security Review*, Cm 7948 (London: The Stationery Office, 2010), paras. 2.4–2.7; Ministry of Defence, *Defence Reform: An independent report into the structure and management of the Ministry of Defence*, Report of the Defence Reform Unit (London: The Stationery Office, June 2011), paras. 1.7–1.8; House of Commons Public Administration Select Committee (PASC), *Who does UK National Security?*, HC 435, 18 October 2011, and HC 713, 28 January 2011.

Inquiry on the Iraq War, for example, was not convened until the UK's Iraq campaign was over. Independent organisations such as RUSI, however, have the freedom, and the duty, to discuss these issues when sufficient research material is available to put some honest perspectives before the public.

Accordingly, we have taken advantage of the fact that several senior military, political and civil service personnel closely involved with the decisions of 2005–06 have retired and are available to speak about the issue, either off the record or in public. The Chilcot Inquiry, and recent evidence to parliamentary committees, have provided some other important material. And some of those involved have published their own accounts, from the battlefield to the centres of command, which also throw new light on the decisions of the key period in 2005–06.

A number of private discussions between small groups of participants took place at RUSI as part of an ongoing research project on the Afghan campaign in September and October 2011. An article published in the *RUSI Journal* in August set out some basic ideas about these decisions and participants at the private meetings were asked to comment.[3] That material was then refined and further meetings arranged. The result, to date, is this collection of papers.

Those written by RUSI researchers arise from private group discussions, personal interviews and new sources of written evidence. These papers seek to analyse the dynamics driving the key decisions. They are intended to help understand the UK's narrative that led to the situation of late summer 2006 when Britain clearly took on a war in Central Asia; to understand the aid and development side of the policy as it evolved; and to set it within the critical perspective of what the US, Canada and the Netherlands were planning as their part of the deployments agreed during 2005.

Other contributors are included here from our ongoing process to gather the perspectives of some of those who were part of the key decisions, or who were in a good position to observe

[3] Michael Clarke and Valentina Soria, 'Charging up the Valley: British Decisions in Afghanistan', *RUSI Journal* (Vol. 156, No. 4, August/September 2011), pp. 80–88.

them as insiders. Serving officers and officials have not been approached to contribute either to the RUSI discussions or to the papers that will subsequently appear in the *RUSI Journal*. But many private conversations have taken place, in and around this work, to try to ensure that recollections and the spectrum of opinions are treated fairly.

A concluding paper reflects on the broader strategic significance of the origins of the UK's Afghan campaign.

The intention of this volume is not to arrive at a definitive judgement on the strategic coherence or the value to the national interest of the UK's campaign in Afghanistan. More evidence covering the whole campaign, and a sense of the outcomes after 2015, will be necessary before that can be attempted. But, in a period of great uncertainty for the UK's defence and security institutions, it is important that the complex reality of policy-making is not caricatured in a series of easy political sound bites, and volumes such as this are intended to throw their weight against casual judgements. The complex reality of the decisions dealt with here does not necessarily favour either the supporters or the opponents of the Afghan campaign. They demonstrate with equal conviction that strategy has to be fashioned from a constant flow of known and unknown events covering issues from different theatres all happening simultaneously; but also that without clear-headed, and timely, intervention in that flow, coherent strategy is unlikely to emerge. The reality of security policy presents a challenge that is at once daunting, but unavoidable.

THE HELMAND DECISION

MICHAEL CLARKE

The United Kingdom's operations in Afghanistan since 2006 have become highly controversial. There have been many accounts of the tactical skill and bravery of UK forces on the ground. Some officers have written their memoirs, journalists have published their accounts of being embedded with the soldiers on the front line, and TV series have revealed a good deal of the reality of life in a theatre of operations.[1] Other accounts, however, have presented the Afghanistan operation as confused in every key respect; a strategic blunder that is heading towards irredeemable failure.[2] The decision to withdraw from combat operations 'by 2015' is seen in these accounts as damage limitation and political expediency, rather than any meaningful completion of the mission.

---

[1] Stuart Tootal, *Danger Close: Commanding 3 PARA in Afghanistan* (London: John Murray, 2009); Max Benitz, *Six Months Without Sundays: The Scots Guards in Afghanistan* (London: Birlinn, 2011); Patrick Bishop, *3 Para* (London: Harper Press, 2007); Chris Terrill, *Commando* (London: Century, 2007). See also BBC2, *Afghanistan: War Without End?*, 22 June 2011 and BBC2, *Afghanistan: The Battle for Helmand*, 29 June 2011.

[2] Frank Ledwidge, *Losing Small Wars: British Military Failure in Iraq and Afghanistan* (New Haven, CT: Yale University Press, 2011); James Fergusson, *A Million Bullets: The Real Story of the British Army in Afghanistan* (London: Corgi Books, 2008), Stephen Jermy, *Strategy for Action: Using Force Wisely in the 21st Century* (London: Knightstone, 2011). See also Theo Farrell, 'Review Essay: A Good War Gone Bad?', and book reviews by Frank Ledwidge and Robert Johnson, in *RUSI Journal* (Vol. 156, No. 5, October 2011).

Whether or not the Afghanistan operation is eventually perceived as a sorry strategic failure, a political success, or perhaps some messy compromise that nevertheless achieves some useful security objectives after 2015, its outcome will have a major effect on the burgeoning debate about strategy – national strategy and military strategy – now underway in the UK.

Afghanistan cannot be divorced from this wider debate. The Afghanistan decisions of 2005 and 2006 are increasingly seen as a significant example of the problem the UK has acknowledged it has in formulating a national strategy and carrying it through with military coherence.[3] In July 2011, the House of Commons Defence Committee published a critical report that expressed deep disquiet about the way the early decisions to engage in Afghanistan seem to have been made. It regarded as 'unacceptable' three years of deployment in Afghanistan that was based on 'a failure of military and political co-ordination'. The implications of initial deployment decisions, it said, were not 'fully thought through'.[4] The report put a good deal of new evidence into the public domain and the Committee also had the benefit of private briefings before drawing its conclusions. In addition, the published evidence of the Chilcot Inquiry, dealing with all aspect of the Iraq operation, involved some witnesses making a number of authoritative statements that also added to the understanding of some of the key Afghan decisions. Military and political writers increasingly express a consensual view that the UK is 'not very good' at strategy and that its politico-military decisions over the last decade have, at best, been less than satisfactory, and, at worst, have let down the men and women who have fought in Iraq and Afghanistan.[5]

---

[3] The debate effectively began with the lecture given by then Chief of the Defence Staff Air Chief Marshal Sir Jock Stirrup, at RUSI, London, 3 December 2009, calling for 'the habit of thinking strategically' among British defence professionals. Available at <http://www.rusi.org/events/past/ref:E4B184DB05C4E3/>.

[4] House of Commons Defence Committee [HCDC], *Operations in Afghanistan*, HC 554, 17 July 2011, paras 28, 67.

[5] See, for example, the reports and evidence of the Public Administration Select Committee [PASC], *Who Does UK National Security?*, HC 435, 18 October 2011, and HC 713, 28 January 2011 (both London: The Stationery Office, 2011).

A detailed discussion of the origins of the UK's Afghan campaign is therefore of some importance in the wider strategic debate. It offers evidence to support both those who argue for the underlying coherence of the UK's strategy in South Asia and Afghanistan, and those who cannot see any real strategic logic in the flow of decisions that were made during the critical early period. Most are agreed that tactical innovation by the armed forces on the ground – learning and adapting, applying new lessons, finding ways to prevail – has been impressive. But good tactics cannot rescue bad strategy; at most they might disguise some of its failings.

Most observers are also agreed that UK forces have struggled to dominate their tactical environment in Afghanistan; rather, they have been playing catch-up in a rapidly changing military (and political) environment. Tactical evolution in Afghanistan has certainly been rapid. The 1,000 or so UK military personnel who had operated with ISAF forces from 2001, mainly in Kabul and in posts in the north, were effectively replaced by a combat force of 3,300 troops in the southern province of Helmand during the spring of 2006. By the autumn of that year their number had jumped to 6,300 troops in theatre, and by July 2007 to almost 7,600. In 2009, the government of Prime Minister Gordon Brown confirmed that, after a temporary increase, the number would be held at 'an enduring maximum of 8,300',[6] but that was quickly exceeded and despite (Brown's successor) Prime Minister David Cameron's troop withdrawals during 2011, numbers in theatre actually peaked at just over 10,000. Even in the current period of drawdown from combat roles, numbers are planned to remain relatively high in the approach to the deadline at the end of 2014.

Of more pressing concern than troop numbers, the threat posed by improvised explosive devices (IEDs) is a good indicator of the changing nature of the operation and the constant difficulty the forces experienced in controlling the tactical environment. IED attacks against UK forces in the province increased steadily from June 2006 to December 2007,

---

[6] HM Government, *UK Policy in Afghanistan and Pakistan: The Way Forward* (London: The Stationery Office, 2009), p. 18.

notwithstanding a temporary fall in the autumn of 2006, reaching peaks of thirty-two attacks in a single month.[7] In the two years after 2006, IED attacks in southern Afghanistan increased fourfold, and then more than twofold again in the following two years up to 2010.[8] By March 2010, 78 per cent of all IED attacks in Afghanistan were in the UK's area of operations and were causing the vast majority of UK military casualties.[9]

This threat, in turn, required the Ministry of Defence to rush into service a number of new mine-resistant vehicles; this has not only created a diverse and expensive fleet to operate, but also effectively put the final nail into the coffin of the army's cherished programme to develop a single, generic medium-weight armoured vehicle for the long-term future.[10] Snatch Land Rovers were immediately unsuitable in Afghanistan. Vector and Mastiff vehicles, introduced in 2007, were also limited; one too light underneath, the other poor in off-road conditions.[11] The Snatch Vixen was introduced in 2008 and then finally, in 2009, a fleet of over 560 new armoured vehicles came into service, including Jackal, Mastiff 2, Ridgeback, Panther, and the tactical support vehicles, Wolfhound, Husky and Coyote.[12]

---

[7] 'Questions by Angus Robertson to Minister of State (Armed Forces) Nick Harvey', *Hansard*, HC Debates, 2 February 2011. Also see Sheila Bird and Clive Fairweather, 'IEDs and Military Fatalities in Iraq and Afghanistan', *RUSI Journal* (Vol. 154, No. 4, August 2009).

[8] *Daily Telegraph*, 'Child Suicide Threat to British Troops', 13 December 2008.

[9] *Independent*, 'Taliban Doubles Number of Bomb Attacks on British Troops', 13 June 2010.

[10] The Future Rapid Effects System (FRES) programme was intended to provide a generic medium-weight vehicle from which many variants could be economically derived for the next generation of armoured, manoeuvre warfare. See for example Olivier Grouille, 'FRES: Alive but Not Quite Kicking', *RUSI Defence Systems* (Vol. 12, No. 1, June 2009).

[11] National Audit Office, *Support to High Intensity Operations*, Report by the Comptroller and Auditor General, HC 508 (London: The Stationery Office, 14 May 2009), p. 13.

[12] *Ibid.*, p. 12.

Such adaptations, and many others, reflect well on the ability of the military, and the Urgent Operational Requirements (UOR) procedures, to address issues such as the IED threat as they have arisen. Despite persistent press speculation over these years that the military were not supplied with all the equipment they subsequently requested, there is no evidence to contradict the assertion of senior commanders and politicians that once the operation was underway no request for equipment was ever turned down.[13] British troops and commanders in Afghanistan are now better equipped than any force the UK has ever fielded anywhere. But the evolution in equipment in these ways was never part of an integrated plan for the future of the forces, and they have created a public image more of improvisation rather than of coherent adaptation.

The key decisions over the Afghanistan campaign have come back to the home front. After so publicly playing catch-up on the ground, it is hardly surprising that domestic public support for the campaign has been tepid and sometimes confused. In 2006, unambiguous public support for the operation stood only at 31 per cent. By 2009, and in a large survey of 20,000 people, it stood at only 18 per cent. Opposition to the operation was running at somewhere between 51 per cent and 56 per cent in 2009 polls.[14]

---

[13] Author interviews 13 and 22 September 2011. Requests from theatre for items under the Urgent Operational Requirements procedure were sent direct to the Chief of Joint Operations at the PJHQ, and thence with a recommendation to the Deputy Chief of Defence Staff (Operations) for approval. The only occasion when a politician intervened, and the only occasion when a request from theatre was delayed, was over the uplift of 500 extra UK troops during the period of the Afghan elections in 2009. There was a two-month delay in confirming the decision while Downing Street sought clarification of the incoming Obama Administration's position on the Afghan elections. Ex-senior officers are adamant that no equipment request from theatre was either refused or delayed at any time after June 2006.

[14] See Thomas J Scotto et al, 'Attitudes Towards British Involvement in Afghanistan', briefing paper, Institute for Democracy and Conflict Resolution, March 2011, p. 4; and also *BBC News*, 'Most Remain against Afghan War', 7 October 2009.

Little wonder that the Conservative-Liberal Democrat coalition government elected in May 2010 was keen to create the trajectory of a guaranteed withdrawal between now and 2015 – something that could be well advanced by the next general election. If Afghanistan is viewed as little more than a national strategic blunder, then a political decision to escape from it as soon as possible is entirely sensible. But if it is viewed as part of a more coherent strategy towards South Asia in general and Afghanistan in particular, then the announcement of withdrawal deadlines runs the risk of fundamentally undermining that politico-military strategy.

There are two plausible interpretations of policy that took UK forces into the situation they found themselves in at the beginning of 2007, moving towards a deployment of over 7,000 troops, coping with a growing IED threat and finding themselves having to learn and adapt quickly to changing circumstances. One emphasises coherent national purposes and the momentum of international commitments; the other emphasises ad hoc decisions and the difficulties of creating a meaningful strategic focus in the face of multiple challenges. The contrast lies between a coherent strategy that reacts to longer-term international trends, and a series of ad hoc and partisan responses that are retrospectively rationalised as a strategy.

A Coherent Strategy: Responding to International Momentum

Viewed in the context of events since 2001, the political intent behind the Afghan policy of the US and its allies could be stated quite succinctly; to expel Al-Qa'ida from the territory of Afghanistan where it had partly hijacked the Taliban government and launched attacks on the US, and then to deny terrorists any ungoverned space in the region for future operations. While the US worked to track down Al-Qa'ida leaders in their counter-terrorism operations around the Afghan border, the allies of the US supported efforts to create some sustainable governance in a post-Taliban Afghanistan that would remove the ungoverned spaces. This was the thinking behind the original International Security Assistance Force (ISAF) mission of December 2001. It expressed the political intent of the US and its allies clearly enough, and the military implications would evolve from that.

By 2002, the line of logic was that the ISAF role could not be performed unless its remit covered the whole country, not just Kabul and areas of the north, as only this would allow the Afghan Transitional Administration to become the post-Taliban government. Thus, when NATO agreed to take over its responsibility for ISAF in early 2003 as a 'nation-building exercise', it embodied the 'clock-face' plan to extend security operations from the north to the west, then to the south, and then finally to the east of the country which would encompass the most vigorous US counter-terrorism efforts. The alternative logic would be to stand by while a barely sustainable Afghanistan effectively split into a Pashtun heartland in the south, extending across the Durand Line border into the Pashtun areas of Pakistan, and an isolated north around Kabul with the western city of Herat probably falling even further under longstanding, historic Iranian influence. Having committed itself to make Afghanistan properly 'governable', the international community had to be prepared ultimately to extend security and development of the whole country in order to leave behind something sustainable. The strategy was based on the apparent success of the Provincial Reconstruction Teams (PRTs) – a concept that the UK had helped to pioneer – to create local development in key areas of the country. The PRTs would be the route to sustainability for a new Afghan government, though they would have to be protected and work in areas that were generally secure. The military would be the servant of the PRTs.

The military component of this strategy, however, remained hard to determine before 2005, since there was no clear idea of how difficult or easy it might be to ensure security across the country – the necessary but not sufficient condition for the governance and development Afghanistan. What was certain, however, was that US troops would ultimately have to be part of the equation, both for their potential numbers and the political weight they carried. The willingness of Washington's allies to put troops on the ground in Afghanistan was, in turn, the pre-requisite for getting US troops into the theatre in some numbers. So the grand strategic argument was simple, and somewhat circular. If Afghanistan was part of the international terrorist problem, it would have to be transformed in some way. The original ISAF plan would fail in this respect, unless it was extended to the whole country. To make this work, US numbers would be required, but in order to trigger this increased deployment, allied nations would have to commit in some serious way. All this, to assist the US in its own strategy and to help NATO's credibility, both in Washington and in Europe.

For the British, however, this logic had particular force. Acting as a focus for such an allied strategic approach, the UK would stay close to the US, helping the Americans see through the strategic logic of their own Afghan policy. It would give the UK opportunities to capitalise on its historic influence with Pakistan, and it would help reinvigorate NATO with a mission that was consistent with the Alliance's more global aspirations. In this last respect, the mission would also validate NATO's Allied Rapid Reaction Corps (ARRC), under UK command, that would run the ISAF mission in the first instance. The ARRC was one of the key sources of UK military influence in the Alliance.

If all this was logical, and better than the alternative of an unsustainable and fractured Afghanistan, there were nevertheless some costs and dangers in this approach. The strategy was necessarily multinational and as such created a momentum of its own for a country such as the UK. Through its size and centrality, the US might have chosen to flip its strategy or do a complete U-turn; and smaller powers, as minor contributors, might have chosen to participate or not. But the UK positioned itself as a significant strategic player in the game and the potential costs of U-turns or irresolute behaviour would be very high indeed. Having engaged with the need to 'do something' about Afghanistan in late 2001, the momentum of multinational action was very hard to escape. The choice appeared to be to let the strategy fail, or engage more with it.

However, the strategy was already saddled with the mistakes the international community made in the very early years; the 2001 Bonn Agreement 'imposed a victor's peace' on the country and excluded key Pashtun figures and Taliban supporters from any role in the new Afghanistan; the US showed itself almost entirely pre-occupied with counter-terrorism operations in Afghanistan, which had the effect from the outset of working against the thrust of the ISAF mission; and the international community was frankly distracted from Afghan concerns at exactly the moment when its influence could have been most constructive. In 2001–02, all attention was on the Indo-Pakistani stand-off following the terror attack on the Indian parliament in Dehli of December 2001, and in 2002–03, the world was gripped by the looming invasion of Iraq.

The NATO plan – the 'clock-face' of progressive engagement throughout Afghanistan – hardly compensated for these disadvantages. It had little to say about development and governance beyond the PRT process. It was, by default, 'the plan' for the international community's already flawed engagement in Afghanistan's future. It became a powerful political driver for military deployment, but it did not exist at a level of detail that was helpful for military planning purposes. It had the effect of driving the process forward, but not acting to co-ordinate between the participating NATO countries.

It might still have been possible to navigate through all of these problems, the argument goes, were it not for the huge distraction of the Iraq invasion in early 2003. This dominated military thinking for the next five or more years and made it very difficult to focus on Afghanistan's needs in the key period between 2003 and 2006. In particular, the US found it almost impossible to focus its attention on events on the ground in Afghanistan, and when UK military leaders were told by their counterparts that US forces would 'follow them in' to Afghanistan – the allies triggering a US commitment to NATO's clock-face strategy – those assurances were either over-interpreted by UK officers or, in effect, reneged upon as the US was drawn further into the Iraqi quagmire of that time.

The Iraq invasion had major consequences for many aspects of global and regional security, and for many critics of UK policy this appears to be more an excuse than a reason. Ultimately, however, the argument that the UK's Afghan engagement was based on a coherent and realistic strategy rests on the foundation that it was part of a necessarily international strategy, with all the limitations and failings implied by that; and that had the UK not engaged, the alternatives would have been worse.

A Rationalised Strategy: Aggregating Lower-Level Decisions

Whatever interpretation is made of the desire to re-engage in Afghanistan from around 2003, there can be little doubt that carrying it through at a time when operations in Iraq so dominated the minds of policy-makers made strategic coherence extremely difficult to maintain by mid-2005. Critical military policy-makers at the time, including military service chiefs, struggle to recall any occasions on which a genuine strategic discussion of the upcoming Afghan commitment took place. Regular meetings and transatlantic video conferences were overwhelmingly dominated by Iraq operations. It was not that policy-makers had no strategic appreciation of the tasks that were about to be undertaken in Afghanistan, but most recall that there were very few opportunities to share them or arrive at a hard-nosed consensus about them.[15]

Three key decisions in particular during this period are difficult to place easily within the coherent 'top-down' model of strategic decision-making: the decision to send UK troops to the province of Helmand, the initial limitation on the force size, and the decision to move the force north from the initial deployment into the platoon houses. It was this last decision that changed the nature of the operation almost overnight.

Sending Troops to Helmand

Some officials have argued since 2005 that if the UK were to commit more forces to Afghanistan, then they should have gone to Kandahar. Sending them to Helmand, they have said, was a strategic error in itself. To make a significant difference, operations in Kandahar, not Helmand, would be most critical. Kandahar was the Pashtun heartland, the place where Taliban influence could be challenged directly, the city and province that really mattered in the struggle to keep Afghanistan united under the authority of a legitimate government in Kabul. Moreover,

---

[15] Author interviews with senior military officials, September 2011.

Kandahar was the natural centre of gravity for British interests in South Asia. The Kandahar-Quetta axis represented one of the key political linkages between Afghanistan and Pakistan, the key trade route, the ideological hub among the southern Pashtun people, and the link that could capitalise on the UK's close and particular relationships with Pakistan.

Nevertheless, the decision to deploy to Helmand appears to have arisen from a prosaic deal among the militaries of three allies. UK forces went to Helmand because the Canadians were determined to go themselves to Kandahar. There had been a Canadian battlegroup in Kandahar since 2002, and then another Canadian deployment to Kabul in 2003, but there was a sense in Ottawa that they were not in a position to make much impact and both the Defence and Foreign Ministries were keen to capitalise on the fact that, after 2004, the British were evidently looking at a further deployment.[16] For its part, the UK was keen to encourage Canadian forces into a more extensive role within the NATO framework. This may be regarded – whether right or wrong – as a strategic judgement for both Ottawa and London. But it arose out of a dual low-level process: between Ottawa and Washington on the one hand; and in a quadripartite military discussion between the US, Canadian, British and Dutch militaries on the other, with the British officer liaising extensively with the Pentagon.[17]

The arrangement that took shape in late 2004 between the military and defence staffs in London, Ottawa and The Hague was that the Canadians would send an enlarged battlegroup to Kandahar; the Dutch would send a battlegroup to the quieter northern flank of Uruzgan province to the north; and the UK would go to the large territories of Helmand. The three allies would be mutually supporting; the UK in the west, the Dutch to their north, and the Canadians to the east. Uruzgan was important to both other provinces because it lay to the accessible north of them. But Helmand and Kandahar were the key. That was where the whole nation-building campaign in the south of Afghanistan would be won or lost in the years to come. In February 2005, just

---

[16] Janice Gross-Stein and Eugene Lang, *The Unexpected War: Canada in Kandahar* (Toronto: Viking Canada, 2007).

[17] Author interview.

prior to the North Atlantic Council meeting that announced NATO's new mission, senior defence officials from Canada and the UK agreed that they had successfully sketched out the way deployments in south Afghanistan would work, but that in Ottawa, at least, it had not so far been put to the prime minister and would still need 'political cover'.[18]

The British were therefore trying to balance a number of elements in 2005: events in southern Iraq were not going smoothly for UK forces; they were working quietly with the Canadians, watching carefully the fraught political debate in The Hague as Dutch parliamentarians threatened to renege on NATO's collective decision to deploy; and had genuine difficulty in getting anyone in the Pentagon to think outside the framework of Iraq.[19] Nevertheless, no evidence has emerged either from documents or interviews that the choice between Helmand and Kandahar was regarded as strategically important by the British. The Foreign Office was content that UK forces should go to Helmand, and Prime Minister Tony Blair was personally keen on the province – the heart of Afghanistan's narco-economy – as that would be consistent with the anti-narcotics lead role, which the UK had accepted in 2001.

The choice of Helmand presented some distinct problems, however. The only coalition forces operating in Helmand at that time were around 100 US special forces on a counter-terrorism mission who had little impact on local people. There was little genuine intelligence available about how benign or hostile an environment it might be for UK forces to enter. Military chiefs did not expect it to be benign – though there is some evidence that the intelligence and civilian agencies thought it might be – but they simply did not know. The distribution of Helmand's population of 1.5 million was considerably different to that of Kandahar; and its local economy worked differently, with different warlords. Poppy production more than doubled in Helmand during 2005–06, and the amount and nature of ground to be covered, in what is easily the largest province in

---

[18] Author interviews.

[19] HCDC, *op. cit.*, Ev. 605. Author interviews.

the country – at around 58,000 km^2, more than three times the size of Wales – was inherently more challenging.

As plans for the deployment progressed, the situation hardly clarified. The intelligence agencies seem to have reported that the Taliban's Quetta Shura had decided to target the British in particular as they arrived in theatre. Pre-deployment planners from 16 Air Assault Brigade, who would lead the UK's first deployment, were reporting back from Helmand that the situation looked very tense and would quickly become relatively hostile – certainly before the brigade was due to reach its full operational capability by July 2006.[20] Brigadier Ed Butler, who led the brigade, has said that he had been told to plan on the assumption of an essentially 'permissive environment' in Helmand, but others have disputed this perception.[21] Planning for allied deployments in the neighbouring provinces was also unclear at this time. The Canadians were finding the task complex, and the commitment of 1,000 Dutch troops was uncertain until as late as 26 January 2006, when the Dutch parliament finally and reluctantly agreed to the operation. At one point, the picture was so confused that the UK chief of the Defence Staff (CDS) halted any further planning until he came under consistent NATO pressure to resume it.[22] Certainly, there was a fractured pre-deployment planning process during 2005 between the planning staff on the ground in Helmand, who were not from 16 Air Assault; the 16 Air Assault planners who were due to go in; the UK's Permanent Joint Headquarters (PJHQ) at Northwood; the UK Ministry of Defence (MoD); NATO's Allied Rapid Reaction Corps planning staff – since they were also deploying as the ISAF headquarters in Kabul; and that being done by other ministries in Whitehall. National planning going on in Ottawa and The Hague was merely another layer of complexity.

---

[20] See also, James Fergusson, *Taliban: The True Story of the World's Fiercest Guerrilla Fighters* (London: Bantam Press, 2010), pp. 133–35.

[21] HCDC, *op. cit.*, para 34.

[22] *Ibid*, para 33.

Limiting the Force Size

Brigadier Butler has reported both publicly and privately that as the scale of the challenge became clearer, at least to him and his 16 Air Assault staff, he asked PJHQ 'on a weekly basis' for more resources; more troops and more enablers – helicopters, electronic assets, vehicles, interpreters, force protection assets, and so on – always to be told that the government had capped force levels at 3,150 troops and that expenditure had been capped at £808 million for a three-year deployment.[23] Even to deploy within the 'lozenge' made up of the triangle between Camp Bastion, Lashkar Gah and Gereshk in central Helmand, and at the outset of the deployment, Butler estimated that he was around 45 per cent short of vehicles of all types; 20 per cent short on support helicopter hours; 11 per cent on attack helicopter hours; and had no flexibility in the C-130 transport fleet, which was already operating at 92 per cent of total capacity.[24] The 'UK Joint Campaign Plan for Helmand' had been written by December 2005 in an inclusive way between all the relevant government departments who would be involved, integrating views and action points from both Kabul and London.[25] But the military component of it, Butler felt, would be difficult, if not impossible, to deliver; and certainly not within the three-year timeframe for which it was written. In January 2006, the MoD's director of operational capabilities (DOC) – outside the dialogue that was going on between 16 Air Assault and PJHQ – began to assess the capabilities involved in the deployment and was working intensively between March and May on a study that independently supported Butler's claims. The DOC's work was

---

[23] *Ibid.*, Ev. 478, para 38; author interview, 19 April 2011. In fact, the 'immovable figure' of 3,150 was lifted to 3,350 when it was realised that Chinook helicopter crews had been omitted from the cap. Even that adjustment had to be agreed by the service chiefs. Butler also pointed out that any capped figure was always 12 per cent lower on any given day because of the normal R&R requirements for individuals, and that before any injuries or illnesses are taken into account.

[24] HCDC, *op. cit.* para 38.

[25] Declassified copy released in June 2011. See John Ware, 'UK's Original Helmand Deployment Plan Examined', *BBC News*, 22 June 2011.

not regarded as 'helpful' to the ongoing deployment process at the time. The DOC's report was submitted to the vice chief of the Defence Staff in July, but it is unclear what then happened to it.[26]

Meanwhile, conditions on the ground in Helmand were getting worse for the deployment. As delays mounted up, the traditional Afghan fighting season drew nearer. There were bumper poppy harvests in 2005 and 2006 and many of the 200,000 casual labourers who drifted into Helmand to pick them were reportedly staying behind to wait for the British to arrive, while local farmers were being told that the British were coming to destroy their crops.[27] US forces had lately antagonised locals in Helmand with preparations for Operation *Mountain Thrust*, a coalition offensive across the south due to begin in mid-May, which far from 'shaping' the operational theatre for the incoming forces, had made it more hostile.[28] Butler was insistent that the deployment was running risks.

Above his level, however, the choices were clear enough; operations in Iraq were absorbing around two-thirds of all deployable resources. Only a single battlegroup was effectively available for Afghanistan and, of course, commanders on the ground always wanted more, but they would have to do the best they could with what was available.

For all practical purposes, the final decision to deploy rested with Defence Secretary John Reid. He had succeeded Geoff Hoon on 5 May 2005, as planning was well underway. He was told, he says, 'that the chiefs had... agreed in principle to a proposal that we would refocus our military efforts from the north to the south of Afghanistan'. He was not comfortable with this ('I didn't care what decision had been taken on principle', he has said) unless he had some assurances from the chiefs.[29] He sought assurances on a number of occasions that the forces being deployed to Helmand would be adequate to the task, and apparently received them from the CDS, General Sir Michael

[26] Author interviews, 19 April and 15 September 2011.

[27] HCDC, *op. cit.*, para 43.

[28] HCDC, *op. cit.*, para 43.

[29] Evidence given to the Chilcot Inquiry by John Reid as Secretary of State for Defence 2005–06, 3 February 2010, Evidence Transcript, p. 55.

Walker. He also sought a written assurance from the CDS as late as September 2005 that the Helmand deployment would still be feasible even if it was impossible to pull more forces out of Iraq. On 19 September a written assurance was agreed between Reid and the CDS to the effect that both the Chief of Joint Operations at PJHQ in Northwood and the Deputy Chief of Defence Staff (Commitments) were content that the Afghan deployment was feasible whatever happened in Iraq.[30] Both those officers, presumably, were basing their judgement on their ability to supply the government-capped force of 3,150 troops that would not cost more than £808 million over three years – not on a deployment that might rapidly have to be reinforced.

Nevertheless, it is evident that assumptions were being made in the MoD that troops and equipment would be coming back from Iraq on a scale that would allow some flexibility in the Afghan deployment, should that prove necessary. But senior ex-officers have confirmed that no detailed staff work was available to give substance to this belief. If a drawdown of forces in Iraq had to be halted or delayed – as it repeatedly was – there was no detailed planning for how the two simultaneous theatres of operation would be manned and supplied.[31]

If Reid was aware of Butler's dialogue with PJHQ and the sparse and contradictory nature of the intelligence picture, he was not obviously affected by it after September 2005. Instead, he laid down three clear pre-conditions that he first revealed publicly to the Chilcot Inquiry on Iraq in 2010. He required more assurances that the costs of the mission would be met in full by the Treasury; that the Canadians would definitely be in place in Kandahar to the east of the British and the Dutch in Uruzgan to the north; and thirdly that the Department for International Development (DfID) would provide sufficient resources for the nation-building activities that would have to follow immediately.[32] He refused to sign off on the deployment for some time, until the end of January

---

[30] *Ibid.*, pp. 58–59.
[31] Author interviews, 13 and 22 September 2011.
[32] Chilcot Inquiry, *op. cit.*, pp. 55–56.

2006, while the situation with the Canadians and the Dutch clarified and while he argued his case in the Afghanistan Group at the Cabinet Office. He is proud of the fact that he did not authorise the deployment until all those conditions were met in early 2006, though, in truth, 16 Air Assault Brigade were struggling to be ready on that timescale in any case.

John Reid's prudence might be regarded as strategic awareness. In some respects it was. Nevertheless, he was dealing with previous decisions that had already been made and acting on assurances that did not affect the essence of the problem. In the event, 16 Air Assault Brigade would have to trust to luck for what it would find in Helmand. There was no scope for a theatre reserve to back up its operations. When the troops deployed into their posts around Lashkar Gah, Gereshk and Camp Bastion in May 2006, they were quickly involved in lethal operations.

The Move North to Platoon Houses

John Reid left the Ministry of Defence on 5 May 2006, to be replaced by Des Browne. Reid claimed that only five weeks later, sitting in the Home Office, he was astonished to hear that UK forces were fighting some desperate battles in isolated platoon houses up in Musa Qala, Sangin, Garmsir, Now Zad and then later in Kajaki, far away from the 'lozenge' of their original deployment. He was not the only one. One British government minister, who should have been in a position to know, subsequently asked a fellow minister in exasperation: 'How the hell did we get ourselves into this position? How did we go charging up the valley without it ever being put to cabinet?'[33] Certainly, the troops had occupied isolated positions, some distance from their intended deployment area in the last week of May; 'fighting for their lives', as Lieutenant General Rob Fry has described it, 'in a series of Alamos in the north of the province'.[34]

This changed an already stretched mission enormously. It put extra pressure on all the key enabling elements for the

---

[33] Author interview, 5 July 2011.

[34] HCDC, *op. cit.*, para 44.

force. Keeping between forty and a hundred soldiers supplied in platoon houses within a hostile environment required even more helicopter hours, more air cover (which was critical that summer) to help beat off attacks, more armoured vehicles, better intelligence, and so on. It dispersed resources that were intended to be operated together. It gave the Taliban, who were known to be concentrating on the British, a series of fixed targets to attack, and it is fortunate that during 2006 they attacked too many places recklessly and failed to concentrate enough fighters decisively to out-gun any one outpost. None of the platoon houses were taken and in the three months between April and June 2006 an independent source estimates Taliban losses at around 1,800 fighters.[35] More significantly, however, platoon houses reduced any room for tactical manoeuvre by Task Force Helmand.[36] The troops could seize very little initiative because they were a thinned-out force locked into static defence – with no theatre reserve to call on. 'The Paras were sent to Sangin for an operation that was supposed to last a few hours, or at most a few days', reports Patrick Bishop. 'As it turned out, the 3 Para battlegroup would be stuck there for the remainder of its time in Helmand.'[37]

Of equal significance is the fact that defence of the platoon houses became highly dependent on close air support; bombing which inevitably isolated and alienated the local population. As on example, the platoon house at Musa Qala called in twenty-six separate air attacks over a ten-day period, directing 249 bombs onto Taliban positions.[38] Not surprisingly, local Afghans were keen to see the troops, no less than the Taliban, leave the area. And when tribal elders in Musa Qala intervened to negotiate a ceasefire around the platoon house, Butler acknowledges that he was probably

---

[35] Bill Roggio, 'Taliban Losses in Afghanistan, Gains in Pakistan', *Long War Journal*, 25 June 2006.

[36] Personalised accounts of the platoon houses in Sangin during that summer can be found in Bishop, *op. cit.*, and of the Royal Marines in Kajaki in Terrill, *op. cit.*, both in Note 1.

[37] Bishop, *op. cit.*, p. 107.

[38] Author interview, 1 April 2011.

within thirty-six hours of having to abandon it because re-supply by Chinook helicopter had become so dangerous.[39] Meanwhile, the more peaceful towns to the south that ought to have been models of secure development became host to disaffected Afghan families fleeing the fighting further north.

This rapid switch in tactics put the UK's operation in Afghanistan onto a different footing. The move into platoon houses not only stretched the force more than had ever been anticipated in London – virtually doubling the number of troops required in theatre inside five months – it created a new series of outposts that could not then be relinquished. Having fought so hard to establish a presence in the north of Helmand, it would be a defeat in the eyes of the Afghan people if these outposts were given up. When the local agreement over Musa Qala broke down, the town had to be retaken from Taliban fighters, and Sangin became the focus for UK military resilience for four years until it was taken over by US marines in September 2010. In that time, some 30 per cent of all UK military casualties were incurred in Sangin and the Upper Sangin Valley.[40]

This switch of tactics has been the source of some controversy for the last five years. A move into the north of Helmand was inevitable at some point. It is an intrinsic part of a counter-insurgency strategy to begin with 'ink spots' and progressively join them up. In this case, however, the troops had barely established themselves in the 'lozenge' around Lashkar Gah, Gereshk and Camp Bastion before moving out. The Taliban had deliberately increased their activity in the northern towns in preparation for the arrival of the British, and Brigadier Butler was faced with the choice of taking them on in

---

[39] *Daily Telegraph*, 'Paras Almost Retreated under Taliban Assault', 2 October 2006. Many interviewees have stressed that the fear of losing a fully laden Chinook in operations to keep Musa Qala supplied, and the political effect that would have, overshadowed everyone's thinking at this time, from the CDS in London to the theatre commanders in Camp Bastion and Kabul.

[40] By the time of the pullout in late September 2010, Sangin had accounted for 106 British fatalities. See *BBC News*, 'UK Troops Leave Helmand's Sangin', 20 September 2010.

the north or letting them come south in circumstances of their own choosing. The platoon house strategy may have been fraught, but it boldly took the fight to the enemy. It was spoken of as an experiment for one month to make a point both to the local population and to the Taliban. Discussions had taken place during April with the Canadian battlegroup in Kandahar as to how the action might be co-ordinated, and Lieutenant Colonel Stuart Tootal, commanding 3 Para, had decided by the second week of May that the time was right to deny the Taliban any uncontested space.[41]

That there was some immediate military logic in moving north was down to the fact that Helmand was already turning into the sort of hostile environment 16 Air Assault had feared it would, but had been equipped only in the hope that it would not. John Reid is clear that when he left the MoD on 5 May 2006 he was leaving behind a classic, counter-insurgency, stabilisation mission. In truth, it was unlikely to be that as long as the Taliban were explicitly gunning for the British; and that was evident to the battlegroup from the beginning of April. In any case, Butler admits that he no longer thought the UK Joint Campaign Plan for Helmand that had been worked out in London was deliverable, and Tootal assumed that establishing control across the province was a prerequisite for any attempt to implement the plan.[42]

The question arises as to whether this was a tactical shift, pure and simple, that responded – as tactics always must – to a changing situation on the ground where any adversary 'has a vote'. Alternatively, it might be interpreted as a tactical shift that nevertheless had major strategic consequences. In this second case, some have regarded it as a tactic that simply followed the long-term logic of a strategy that sent a small force into Helmand in the first place; whether they fought a counter-insurgency battle now or later was immaterial to the fact that, contrary to initial hopes, they would have to fight it at some point. Others have regarded the move to platoon houses as a tactic which had the

---

[41] Bishop, *op. cit.*, p. 49.

[42] Some interviewees have reported that he was indifferent to the whole concept of the plan; others that he simply put the fighting military logic first, given the Taliban activity he observed.

effect of shifting a sustainable strategy – to stay in the 'lozenge' and build from there – to an unsustainable one which pitted a small force in an open fight against an elusive enemy across a big and difficult area.

The Strategic Problem

These judgements raise important questions about the coherence of the UK's strategy and the locus of responsibility for making it and carrying it through. But the fundamental nature of the 'strategy problem' has been obscured in this case by a different *force majeure* which, in itself, is sufficient to explain the platoon houses. The critical element is the role of the governor of Helmand, Mohammed Daoud, who, under predominantly British pressure, had been appointed in December 2005 to replace the manifestly corrupt governor Sher Mohammed Akhundzada. Daoud did not have the power to 'fix' Helmand, both legally and illegally, as Akhundzada had, but he was more honest and certainly hard-working. He had some influence with President Karzai, though not as much as his predecessor, and the British invested a great deal of political capital in his reputation and success.

Governor Daoud was determined that UK forces must move to the north. As long as a single black Taliban flag flew over any Helmand village, he repeatedly said, he had no authority and would lack political force throughout the province.[43] Moreover, he professed to be profoundly disappointed with the UK troops that had been sent to Helmand. He had expected 3,000 front-line warriors to be available – rather than the few rifle companies (around 650 bayonets) with a big support function and a long logistics tail that were provided. He made his views clear at every opportunity; he had Karzai reinforce the message; he demanded high-level personal protection, and implied that he would throw the British out of the province if they could not make their presence felt. He was a prickly partner to work with, but there was a certain logic to his arguments that the British accepted. And

[43] Bishop, *op. cit.*, pp. 110–11.

if their military credibility with Daoud and Karzai was severely damaged, UK forces would have lost half the battle in any case.

In and of itself, this local political pressure created a sense of inevitability for a 'charge up the valley' until it appeared to be an entirely routine matter, not much more than an operational adjustment. It is not the case that the military somehow kept the switch to itself, still less that it was engineered only at the local level in Helmand. The regular liaison network was already extensive. Local officials from DfID and the Foreign Office understood the logic; there were meetings with the Helmand Executive Group and the PRT in Lashkar Gah. The regional headquarters in Kandahar was involved, as well as the Kabul Steering Group chaired by the British ambassador. There was daily contact with PJHQ and weekly teleconferences with the MoD in London.[44]

The actual decision was Brigadier Butler's. He was the man on the ground; it was up to him, and there is a high degree of deference in the British system to back the judgement of the commander in-theatre. But if the responsibility remains with him, it was not a decision he took alone, or without extensive consultation. In the military and political position in which he found himself, it might have been harder to resist the move north than to make it.

The most remarkable feature of this particular decision is the way London seems to have dealt with it. Both John Reid and Des Browne, as successive defence ministers at just that moment in May 2006, have claimed that they only knew about the move north retrospectively. John Reid acknowledges that this had been discussed in previous meetings while he was still defence minister, but always on the basis that a move north would be 'unsustainable' and that Governor Daoud should be discouraged

---

[44] The Helmand Executive Group formed the nucleus of the Provincial Reconstruction Team, made up of officials from the Foreign Office, the military and the British Embassy Drugs Team, and headed by a regional co-ordinator from the Foreign Office. See also HCDC, *op. cit.*, Ev. 497, 498.

from any gesture politics along these lines.[45] The chiefs of staff had certainly been briefed on this possibility on 3 May – though John Reid insists that in his final meeting with the chiefs on that day, two days before he left for the Home Office, it was never an operational option.[46] He has always said that it was four or five weeks later, in his new Home Office post, that he realised how serious a shift in tactics had occurred.[47] Des Browne, who replaced John Reid on 5 May, was taken by the CDS on a rapid visit to UK forces in Iraq on 17 May and in Afghanistan on 18 May. It was a whirlwind orientation for the new minister and it took place amid daily troop losses – eight since he had taken over. Both he and the CDS spent time with Brigadier Butler almost two weeks before the move north and received a briefing on it. Nevertheless, he told the HCDC that he was briefed about it only 'retrospectively', and 'informed by those in command that, in military terms, this was an operational decision'.[48]

There is an important politico-military disconnection here. John Reid saw all the same documents as the military chiefs; he participated in earlier meetings where the proposal to move north was discussed, but he says he regarded their discussions on this topic as somehow unreal; limited only to the need to dampen Governor Daoud's enthusiasm for a northern offensive. Yet the chiefs evidently did not regard the proposal to move north as merely theoretical, unless they thought that everyone on the ground in Helmand, Kandahar and Kabul was fooling themselves. But in the reality of operations, it is quite plausible to believe that meetings of the chiefs in London with John Reid, overwhelmingly dominated as they were by Iraq, a multitude of other issues, and presentational agendas for a disgruntled public, allowed individuals to walk away with different perceptions about the importance of the tactical shift and what was really at stake. Des Browne, too, was obviously briefed, in-theatre, about the operation and was certainly told what it involved. But equally plausibly, although he was told what was going to happen two

[45] HCDC, *op. cit.*

[46] *Ibid.*, para 51; and private briefing with author.

[47] HCDC, *op. cit.*, para 45.

[48] *Ibid.*, para 50.

weeks before it did, he was new in the job, at the end of a gruelling foreign trip and preoccupied with almost daily deaths of British servicemen. It would not be surprising if the technical strategic significance of what he was being told passed him by.

Both ex-ministers have sought to distance themselves in time from the platoon house decision – asserting that they only knew about it 'retrospectively'. This is not consistent with the recollections of senior military officers. But it is also the case that the military chiefs themselves, and other senior officers, have differing recollections not of what they knew about the proposal to move north, but of how they themselves appreciated its significance at the time. The result seems to have been that everyone, politicians and military, knew something about the platoon house tactic, but had varying interpretations of what it really represented.

Throughout this period, from the beginning of 2005 until the late summer of 2006, when the UK clearly had a small war on its hands in Helmand province, the decision-making system seems to have operated in such a way that strategic appreciation rested everywhere and nowhere.

* * * *

These are troubling recollections from a number of those who were involved in the UK's re-commitment to Afghan operations in 2005–06. Viewed from the perspective of the 9/11 attacks, the US determination to remove the Taliban government from Afghanistan and all that flowed from that single determining factor in the political equation, it is evident that there was a powerful momentum in the press of events once a decision to engage in Afghanistan had been taken. On the British side that decision was taken almost instinctively at prime ministerial level by Tony Blair in September 2001. Whatever the Americans did in response to the 9/11 attacks, the British would, one way or another, be alongside them.[49] As one former chief of the Defence Staff has observed, 'Maximum policy choice exists at the point at

---

[49] Tony Blair, *A Journey* (London: Hutchinson, 2010).

which you decide to engage'; thereafter you have to 'see it through' and international momentum progressively limits the available policy options.[50] So on this basis, the intention to re-engage with a failing Afghan campaign in 2003 – to rescue it with a NATO commitment and trigger a new US interest in seeing the Afghan policy through – has some consistency and strategic coherence about it. Whether or not it comes to be seen as a good strategic instinct will be a judgement for history. Certainly, the mission has not yet failed, even if it is facing some severe challenges.

Nevertheless, it is hard to find this consistent rationale at work throughout the policy machinery in the critical eighteen months between early 2005 and summer 2006. As participants have variously recorded, what thinking could be spared for Afghanistan from the preoccupation with Iraq centred much more on getting the force there than on what would happen once it was operating. In the absence of a detailed and convincing campaign plan for the whole of the Afghan campaign, lower-level decisions certainly had strategic consequences and, in some cases, may have been strategic by default. So the decision to send a small force to Helmand, as opposed to sending a larger force (and perhaps to Kandahar) left the success of the mission to be determined by fate more than usual. And the decision to move north so quickly with only small forces, created a dynamic of mission-creep which may or may not have been inevitable, but which certainly left the troops struggling to impose themselves on the operational space – having to play catch-up until relatively recently. Given that the genesis of the British commitment in 2005 goes back to decisions taken four years earlier, and in an international climate that was so fraught and volatile, it is not surprising that this campaign has become difficult to interpret in national strategic terms. For both good and bad, however, it will be seen as replete with lessons that must be learnt, or re-learnt, for the future.

---

[50] Personal interview, 13 September 2011.

FLAWED 'COMPREHENSIVENESS': THE JOINT PLAN FOR HELMAND

VALENTINA SORIA

In 2006, the UK committed itself to a course of action in southern Afghanistan that was soon to prove unsustainable. A rapid deterioration of security conditions on the ground forced the military to take the fight to the enemy and to extend the scale of its kinetic operations. Tactical and operational decisions took on strategic significance and ultimately upset UK efforts in Helmand Province.

The original assumption was that the UK would embark on a stabilisation and reconstruction mission, which would entail very few – if any – combat operations alongside a rather extensive political and developmental engagement. This rationale underpinned the government's campaign-planning at the time and, crucially, affected the shape and substance of the subsequent UK deployment in the region. As dramatic events unfolded throughout the summer of 2006, it became progressively clear that the UK's initial approach had been largely aspirational and overly optimistic; accordingly, the strategy that had been envisaged soon turned out to be unachievable.

At the time of its conception in 2005, the Joint Plan for Helmand was perceived as a real opportunity to contribute to a far-reaching and effective UK strategy for nation-building which would coherently link together security, assistance, developmental and economic lines of activity, thereby being genuinely cross-governmental in character. This was all the more compelling from a UK perspective since the Iraqi experience post-2003 had highlighted the shortcomings of the country's approach to the so-called 'Phase 4' of conflict; that is, the stabilisation and reconstruction stage. Indeed, it has been argued that no clear 'end state' was identified for the Iraqi theatre prior to intervention and that an overall campaign plan for the post-invasion period was not properly formulated.[1]

The Joint Plan for Helmand was to address these failings identified from Britain's experience in Iraq by incorporating and promoting the kind of holistic approach required in the context of modern conflict. Yet, although underpinned by a sound philosophy, its potential was undermined from the outset by a flawed planning mechanism which defied the very principle of 'jointness' that it was supposed to pursue, as well as by a poor institutional insight (and foresight) capability, which prevented the development of a sustainable implementation plan.

These shortcomings became even more apparent as soon as the decision was taken to conduct aggressive military operations across the province. The subsequent move to the north of Helmand Province, it has been argued,[2] completely derailed the Joint Plan by fundamentally upsetting the strategic terms of reference of the UK's deployment, invalidating some of the critical assumptions upon which the plan itself had been built. Even before that initiative, though, the ambitious endeavour was already undermined in principle by an inadequate operational and logistical infrastructure.

The 'charge up the valley' was the final nail in the coffin but, as originally conceived, the UK's Joint Plan for Helmand was perhaps destined to fail from its inception.

---

[1] Witness statement by Tim Cross to the Chilcot Inquiry, 7 December 2009.

[2] Author interview with government officials, October 2011. See also James Fergusson, *A Million Bullets: The Real Story of the British Army in Afghanistan* (London: Corgi Books, 2008), p. 217.

The (Missed) Lessons of Iraq

The decision to deploy in Helmand Province to support the NATO expansion plan in southern Afghanistan provided the UK with a real opportunity to make amends for what had gone wrong during the stabilisation and reconstruction phase of the Iraqi campaign. Indeed, such experience offered valuable lessons that, if properly incorporated at the time, could have effectively recalibrated the UK's comprehensive approach. First and foremost, the UK's effort in Iraq was undermined from the outset by poor intelligence collection and interpretation, which meant that British troops deployed with an inadequate contextual understanding. This explained, in part, the misplaced expectation of finding a generally permissive security environment, with a local population that, planners believed, would welcome foreign troops as liberators.

Even more worryingly, the Iraqi theatre highlighted the inability of the upper echelons of the UK's institutional system to think about, and prepare for, the post-war effort.[3] In the view of many officials,[4] this translated into a failure of imagination and planning with regards to the level and kind of resources necessary to carry out both the security and reconstruction effort. Accordingly, a situation developed where the military operations to 'clear' areas could not be sustained as the number of available troops was too small, and could not be properly exploited because the efforts were not followed through. The inability to improve the living conditions of the local population quickly and visibly in turn made the 'Hold' phase increasingly difficult to sustain.

This was partly the result of what Daniel Korski identifies as strong resistance in the British system to greater civil-military partnership, which resulted in a very limited developmental input into the Iraqi post-war strategy.[5] To compound this,

[3] Richard Teuten and Daniel Korski, *Preparing for Peace: Britain's Contribution and Capabilities*, Whitehall Paper 74 (London: Routledge/ RUSI, 2010), p. 35.

[4] Author interviews with former MoD officials (September 2011) and current DfID official (October 2011).

[5] Daniel Korski, 'British Civil-Military Integration: History and Next Steps', *RUSI Journal* (Vol. 154, No. 6, December 2009), p. 16.

cultural and conceptual differences meant that for a long time the MoD, Foreign Office and DfID had found it extremely hard to communicate with, let alone understand, each other. A number of former officials connected with the process have tended to argue that the difficulty in agreeing a common set of objectives was the result of a reluctance to work together, due in turn to a desire to maintain a position of institutional primacy.[6] In the case of DfID and the Foreign Office, for example, the desire to keep control of civilian deployments in specific missions and posts also characterised the initial stage of the Helmand campaign and was to manifest itself in their approach towards both the Post Conflict Reconstruction Unit (PCRU) and the Provincial Reconstruction Team (PRT), established on the ground in February 2006.[7] DfID in particular had concerns about ceding authority for development activities to a Foreign Office-led PRT. This attitude was the result of both a desire to keep control of financial resources devoted to developmental/reconstruction activities and a genuine concern related to the best allocation of such resources on the ground. From DfID's perspective, a tension existed between military pressures to concentrate available resources on the development of Helmand Province, and the DfID view that local governance could only be improved by strengthening the central government's capabilities.[8] Over time, DfID recognised that a greater direct investment at the provincial level was needed to facilitate extension of the central government's remit to Helmand.

A similar attitude towards the PCRU was also shared by the Foreign Office. Unlike the MoD, which viewed it as a tool to improve coherence among the civilian departments, some in the Foreign Office perceived the unit as a 'challenge' to their institutional position, in that its very creation could be seen as pointing to a failure on its part to perform all of what it saw as its responsibilities and guarantee the level of co-ordination that had been lacking in Iraq but would be crucial in Afghanistan.[9]

---

[6] Author interviews with DfID and MoD officials, October 2011.

[7] *Ibid.*

[8] *Ibid.*

[9] *Ibid.*

Multiple Goals for Just One Plan

Against the backdrop of such inter-departmental tension, it is no wonder that the 2005 Joint UK Plan for Helmand was never truly 'joined-up', for it could not have been the expression of an optimised collaborative approach which simply did not exist at the time. Cross-governmental consultations certainly did take place, but they could not lead to a seamless incorporation of individual departmental plans – a reflection of conflicting, and to some extent irreconcilable, priorities and objectives. DfID, for instance, has traditionally conceived its role in 'poverty reduction' terms, in line with the International Development Act of 2002. Such a mandate means that DfID usually works in post-conflict areas, rather than in countries where hostilities may still be ongoing, with considerable implications for the conditions of deployment of its civilian staff, their specific remit, and the type of activities they are expected to carry out. Over time, this may have contributed to the encouragement of an institutional culture of reluctance to work in countries at risk,[10] where civilian-led reconstruction activities need to go hand in hand with military-led counter-insurgency aimed at clearing contested areas and providing acceptable levels of security. The criticism often voiced by military officers that 'DFID personnel preferred to work around a conflict rather than on it'[11] seems to suggest, therefore, that in 2005–06 DfID did not have the required attitude and type of resources to work in a semi-permissive (or hostile) environment, as indeed Helmand Province turned out to be only a few months into the UK's deployment. Up to that point, DfID staff were getting little of the specific training needed to operate in such a scenario – which both explains the scarcity of civilian resources on the ground and contributed to the lack of flexibility of those who had deployed. Some have argued that at the time DfID did not give enough

---

[10] House of Commons Defence Committee [HCDC], *The Comprehensive Approach: The Point of War is not Just to Win but to Make a Better Peace*, Seventh Report of Session 2009–10, HC 224 (London: The Stationery Office, March 2010), p. 27.

[11] Theo Farrell and Stuart Gordon, 'COIN Machine: The British Military in Afghanistan', *RUSI Journal* (Vol. 154, No. 3, June 2009), p. 24.

priority to finding an adequate pool of suitable people to send and do the job.[12] This may have reduced DfID's ability to provide sufficient support to the UK's overall effort in the province.

An even greater tension existed between counter-insurgency on the one hand and counter-narcotics on the other. The UK had taken on the counter-narcotics commitment from the beginning of the ISAF campaign and the mission soon became a Foreign Office priority. The Foreign Office grew even more determined to carry it out effectively when the UK took responsibility for Helmand, the centre of Afghan opium production. To this end, in 2005 the Foreign Office pushed hard for the removal of the Helmand governor, Sher Mohammed Akhundzada, a very controversial figure with solid connections to local drug dealers.[13]

However, in 2006 the military found it hard to see the case for giving support to the counter-narcotics mission and, in fact, were never part of it. They were concerned that a poppy-eradication strategy would alienate the local population, with the risk of fuelling the very insurgency they were trying to stifle. As pointed out by Brigadier Ed Butler, then commander of 16 Air Assault Brigade, the military 'took a tactical view that we couldn't get involved in those [counter-narcotics operations] because we could see that that was the quickest way of upsetting the ordinary Afghan farmer. We didn't want to turn the farmer into an insurgent, so counter-narcotics was another contradictory objective'.[14] From this perspective, even Akhundzada's removal must have been seen as particularly untimely insofar as it dramatically destabilised the tribal balance of power in the province and eliminated what had been, up to that point, a stabilising factor. There is no doubt that the replacement of such a corrupt figure was a mandatory step on the road towards improving local governance and the national government's

[12] Author interview with DfID official, October 2011.

[13] See James Fergusson, *op. cit.*, p. 208 and Thomas Schweich, 'Is Afghanistan a Narco-State?', *New York Times*, 27 July 2008.

[14] Evidence by Ed Butler to the HCDC, *Operations in Afghanistan*, Fourth Report of Session 2010–12, HC 554 (London: The Stationery Office, July 2011), Ev. 103.

accountability. Yet, the repercussions of this decision, and of the broader counter-narcotics agenda, on the viability of the counter-insurgency campaign were not fully appreciated. This reveals a disturbing lack of cross-department policy discussion at the time as to the implications of pursuing the two missions concurrently.[15]

Drafting the Plan

In 2005, two crucial factors caused the Joint Plan to be based on weak foundations: an 'information vacuum' and a diversion of resources away from Afghanistan caused by the UK's concurrent commitment in Iraq.[16]

Prior to 2006, Helmand Province had been substantially untouched by allied military operations and the only significant military activity on the ground was the US counter-terrorism offensive conducted by US Special Forces and aimed at eliminating members of Al-Qa'ida. The US had also established a small PRT unit, but it acted on the principle of 'economy of force',[17] which meant that the number of civilian and military personnel combined did not amount to more than 300.[18] As a consequence, their engagement with the local population was very limited and the intelligence picture acquired was accordingly poor.

Unable to rely on the US experience to develop a reliable understanding of the local environment, the UK sent out a small special forces reconnaissance mission to gather relevant intelligence, which would then be used to draft a sound strategic plan. According to Peter Wall, then deputy chief of joint operations at Permanent Joint Headquarters (PJHQ), the

---

[15] James Fergusson, *op. cit.*, p. 230.

[16] House of Commons Foreign Affairs Committee, *Global Security: Afghanistan and Pakistan*, Eighth Report of Session 2008–09 (London: The Stationery Office, July 2009), p. 85.

[17] Stuart Gordon, 'Winning Hearts and Minds? Examining the Relationship between Aid and Security in Afghanistan's Helmand Province', Feinstein International Center, Tufts University, April 2011, p. 31.

[18] The number of civilians was in fact in double figures.

intelligence collection task was viewed by PJHQ very seriously, in light of the far from satisfying performance in Iraq.[19]

However, the amount and quality of intelligence acquired in the short timeframe preceding the UK's deployment did not allow for a thorough appreciation of the complex tribal, social and political dynamics of the province. The intelligence community has been criticised for failing to provide a trusty analysis of the real state of the Taliban insurgency,[20] which led to an underestimation of the threat and fuelled a sense of misplaced confidence in Whitehall as to what could be achieved. Others, however, suggest that the intelligence picture was as good as it could get: it was certainly limited, and it could not have anticipated how conditions would change as a consequence of the arrival of UK troops;[21] it did not appear to be contradictory, though, and was appropriate for the type and limited geographical extension of the reconstruction mission originally envisaged.[22]

But this latter view is at variance with what the preliminary operations team was reporting back in late 2005. This unit – comprising personnel from DfID, the Foreign Office, PCRU and PJHQ – was tasked with producing the UK's Joint Plan. In December of that year this group was warning Whitehall that they did not in fact know enough to come up with a sustainable, long-term plan for Afghanistan. During their three-month deployment in Helmand between January and March 2006, it also became increasingly apparent to them that the province was already in a state of crisis.[23] Yet, in the meantime, the Joint Plan had been approved for delivery in a three-year timeframe, with a

---

19 Evidence by Peter Wall to the HCDC, *Operations in Afghanistan, op. cit.*, Ev. 144.

20 Deborah Haynes, 'They Went into Helmand with Eyes Shut and Fingers Crossed', *The Times*, 9 June 2010.

21 Evidence by Richard Reid to the HCDC, *Operations in Afghanistan, op. cit.*, Ev. 96.

22 Evidence by Robert Fry to the HCDC, *Operations in Afghanistan, op. cit.*, Ev. 96.

23 Evidence by Ed Butler to the HCDC, *Operations in Afghanistan, op. cit.*, Ev. 105.

budget of £808 million and the number of troops capped at 3,150.

Not enough time was given to a detailed investment appraisal,[24] which might have created a more realistic match between goals, ways and means: yet, such an appraisal would have been difficult to initiate until UK troops had deployed in the province.[25] Only then would it have been possible to realise the real scale of the challenge ahead and to plan accordingly, with due appreciation of the type of end state which was indeed achievable and the kind of campaign that was to be pursued.

The PCRU had been advising a more cautious approach as more time was needed to figure out exactly what the mission should be about, and, accordingly, what kind and level of resources were necessary to execute it. [26] But there was little appetite in London to pause and carry out a thorough analysis;[27] the result was that valuable discussions to raise all the potential challenges that the mission would present were never seen as a priority in Whitehall. Many of those issues had been preliminarily identified in December 2005 by the joint team on the ground,[28] but there was never the opportunity to address them effectively before the actual deployment in April. The unwillingness to go beyond the plan as it was and to spell out a more detailed implementation plan meant that it was not possible to appreciate the difficulties associated with the delivery of certain planned activities.[29] As a consequence, no valid contingency planning, with the view of adapting the original plan to changing circumstances on the ground, was contemplated.

To compound this, there was the fact that the PCRU-led team certainly had some military insight, but lacked full access to

---

[24] *Ibid.*

[25] It is worth pointing out that the Preliminary Operation Team wanted to conduct more granular planning but there was not sufficient appetite for this in Whitehall at the time.

[26] Haynes, *op. cit.*

[27] Author interview with former MoD official, October 2011.

[28] Evidence by Ed Butler to the HCDC, *The Comprehensive Approach*, *op. cit.*, Ev. 15.

[29] Author interview with DfID official, October 2011.

the extent of expertise for what would become a very complex counter-insurgency environment. Indeed, although elements from PJHQ were part of the preliminary operations unit, Task Force Helmand, and more precisely 16 Air Assault Brigade, was not sufficiently represented. This could be explained by the view that the military should not take the lead in a politically-led reconstruction mission, given the prevailing assumption was that the environment would be benign and the level of security sufficient for civilians to carry out reconstruction activities without the need for much military intervention.[30]

Eventually, this decision turned out to be a huge mistake for two connected reasons: first of all, the unit did not have the capability to foresee the tactical implications that the deployment of a foreign military force would have for the nature, and speed, of the resurgent resistance.[31] One could hardly blame the PCRU for failing to do the military's planning for it, but the sheer uncertainty of the security situation on the ground in Helmand made it impossible for the unit to tell the military in any detail what levels of security were necessary for the reconstruction mission to succeed.

Accordingly, 16 Air Assault chose instead to work on their own planning, primarily because they recognised that the Joint Plan was based on a number of unrealistic assumptions which made it undeliverable.[32] The split between the planning team and those who were supposed to implement the plan itself highlights clearly the dysfunctional nature of the planning process and might explain sufficiently why, as has been suggested,[33] the military unit first deployed in the province had, in fact, never bought into the plan. Whether or not this was the case, the end result was a disjointed UK strategy made up of contrasting plans with different prioritisation of several lines of activity pursued on the ground. The inevitable misalignment between military and development activities would then result in

---

[30] Author interview with former MoD official, September 2011.

[31] Fergusson, *op. cit.*, p. 251.

[32] Evidence by Ed Butler to the HCDC, *Operations in Afghanistan*, *op. cit.*, Ev. 107.

[33] Fergusson, *op. cit.*, p. 241.

the sort of tension between the reconstruction and counter-insurgency missions that characterised the initial stages of the UK's Helmand campaign.

The 2005 Joint Plan for Helmand presented severe shortcomings at the strategic, operational and logistical level.[34] Too ambitious in principle, it did not provide a sound implementation plan to link those political aspirations and the operational requirements necessary to realise them. Furthermore, the rushed, ill-considered process characterising the planning phase did not provide the Foreign Office and DfID with enough time to 'staff up' the UK PRT,[35] leading to a shortage of civilian personnel ready to deploy. On the other hand, it is also important to ask whether there had been enough willingness on the part of the civil servants tasked with planning the move into Helmand to talk truth to power and to voice forcefully opposition to a plan that was evidently far too aspirational from the outset. A sense prevailed across the upper echelons of government in 2005 that Afghanistan would provide the opportunity to redeem the UK for its errors in Iraq, by providing a truly comprehensive approach. In such a climate, it was perhaps hard to contradict a course of action that, some felt,[36] the UK had already committed to politically.

Nonetheless, the consequence was that the country embarked on an overly ambitious Afghan campaign at a time when it was still heavily committed in Iraq, both materially and intellectually. Iraq continued to represent the priority theatre and to be perceived as the hardest challenge. It was therefore very easy to underestimate the Afghan endeavour. Moreover, there had not been enough time to incorporate all the lessons identified from Iraq. The process of institutional learning, which should have allowed the Helmand campaign to be a 'success story', had in fact not yet taken place.

---

[34] The view inside DfID is that the plan itself was not allowed to go into the level of detail that would have been necessary to address logistical issues.

[35] 'Global Security: Afghanistan and Pakistan', *op. cit.*, p. 85.

[36] Haynes, *op. cit.*

Implementing the Original Plan and the Subsequent Move to the North

The rationale underpinning the implementation of the Joint Plan was that of the 'ink-spot' strategy, successfully employed by British forces in various counter-insurgency campaigns before.

By committing to a 'concentration of force' principle, the strategy envisaged the establishment of a 'security lozenge' around Helmand's provincial capital, Lashkar Gah, where initial developmental and reconstruction projects were to be delivered. It was assumed that such initiatives would generate positive 'spill-over' effects that,[37] over time, would have allowed the expansion of the British military and civilian presence beyond the town itself so as to gradually transform the political, economic and social landscape of the entire province. As pointed out by General Sir Robert Fry, the whole of the Task Force Helmand, and its supporting infrastructure, sent out to Afghanistan was predicated upon this relatively limited definition of the mission.[38] In other words, key strategic planners were confident at the time that the capped level of troops (3,150) would have been sufficient to sustain the civilian-led reconstruction mission as originally conceived on the assumption that the permissive nature of the local environment would not have required the military to embark on sustained, aggressive 'Clear' operations.[39] Butler confirmed that 'the tactical mission was to deploy the force and establish our footprint',[40] while the expansion phase would be undertaken once the Task Force had reached full operational capability in July 2006.[41] However, the actual situation on the ground during the first few months of the UK deployment soon invalidated the planned timescale, given the more immediate kinetic response that followed.

---

[37] Farrell and Gordon, *op. cit.*, p. 20.

[38] Evidence by Robert Fry to the HCDC, *Operations in Afghanistan*, *op. cit.*, Ev. 91.

[39] Author interview with former MoD official, September 2011.

[40] Evidence by Ed Butler to the HCDC, *Operations in Afghanistan*, *op. cit.*, Ev. 105.

[41] *Ibid.*

Indeed, even before the decision to 'charge up the valley' was taken, security conditions on the ground were steadily deteriorating, as a result of the unforeseen combination of several factors: the poppy-eradication strategy which was depriving Afghan farmers of their unique source of livelihood without providing a valid and sustainable economic alternative; the concurrent re-start of the fighting season, which could rely on an unprecedented availability of workforce because of the British counter-narcotics strategy; and the removal of governor Akhundzada, a move that crucially upset the balance of power in the province.[42] Faced with the inevitable prospect of a much stronger Taliban insurgency, the military realised that the battle to 'clear' the area was indeed inevitable.[43] This meant that, contrary to initial expectations, the limited number of troops available had to be both deployed and employed.[44]

To further exacerbate the situation, the new governor of Helmand, Mohammad Daoud, soon demanded British forces extend the range of their kinetic action to Musa Qala and Sangin in the north of the province, where the local government's authority was being successfully challenged by the Taliban presence. The move northwards that ensued left the military completely overstretched and unable to provide their civilian counterparts with the protective envelopes that they needed to do their job. The Joint Plan was thus shelved before it was ever rolled out. This raises the question: did this occur as a direct result of the move to the north, or was it inevitable from the outset?

The 'charge up the valley', and the subsequent use of the 'platoon house' tactic, represented a significant step away from the original civilian-led reconstruction mission, implying a strategic shift that affected the very nature of the UK's Helmand campaign. This resulted in an inevitable acceleration of the

---

[42] Evidence by Nicholas Houghton to the HCDC, *Operations in Afghanistan*, *op. cit.*, Ev. 144–45.
[43] Fergusson, *op. cit.*, p. 251.
[44] Evidence by Ed Butler to the HCDC, *Operations in Afghanistan*, *op. cit.*, Ev. 106.

military lines of operation ahead of the civilian-led ones,[45] which fuelled the suspicion that the military had abandoned the Joint Plan without genuinely trying to implement it.[46] The move to the north, the argument goes, ultimately derailed the original plan.

On the other hand, the military complained that DfID staff reluctance to initiate reconstruction and development activities in areas that had been relatively secured frustrated any reasonable attempt to consolidate the temporary tactical victories that their offensive was winning.[47] According to this view, civilian reconstruction should have been conceived as a useful 'follow-on force' designed to further enable military operations across the region.[48] It is not difficult to see how this sort of concept of operations that was adopted came to be strongly opposed by the civilian departments that had signed up to the Afghan campaign on the assurance it would be a politically-led effort.

The civil-military friction that characterised the UK's effort in Helmand in 2006 can partly be explained by deep-rooted institutional dispositions, which determined the different organisational attitudes towards what should be given priority in COIN missions. The most evident manifestation of this tension was the difficulty in reconciling and co-ordinating, on the one hand, quick-impact projects (QIPs) that the military favoured, and long-term reconstruction activities on the other. It has been suggested that this might have been the by-product of the varying lengths of rotation periods for civilian and military personnel in theatre – which are usually shorter for the latter.[49] The military tended to view QIPs as the fastest way to visibly improve the economic and living conditions on the ground and, for this reason, they perceived these projects to

[45] Evidence by Ed Butler to the HCDC, *The Comprehensive Approach*, *op. cit.*, Ev. 17.

[46] Fergusson, *op. cit.*, p. 241.

[47] Evidence by Ed Butler to the HCDC, *The Comprehensive Approach*, *op. cit.*, Ev. 17.

[48] Farrell and Gordon, *op. cit.*, p. 24.

[49] Author interview with former Foreign Office official, September 2011. See also evidence by Stephen Grey and Daniel Korski to the HCDC, *The Comprehensive Approach*, *op. cit.*, Ev. 55.

be the most effective tool to win over the local population. Yet, their impact was necessarily limited in time and space, meaning that they could not provide a solid base for the establishment of endurable state governance capabilities. This would have required the sort of long-term commitment that civilian departments were keener to adopt, but that was largely criticised by their military counterparts as being one of the reasons for the UK's failure to exploit the 'hundred days' window of opportunity after the initial conflict,[50] similar to the course of previous events in Iraq.

This failure was largely due to the absence of a strategic plan coherently linking security and aid in a semi-permissive (or still-hostile) environment.[51] Before Iraq and Afghanistan, the tradition had been for civilian-led development and reconstruction missions to be undertaken in post-conflict areas, where, it could be assumed, a reasonable degree of security would be in place, allowing civilian teams to deploy and work on the territory. This inevitably shaped their risk threshold and led both the Foreign Office and DfID to establish specific duty-of-care arrangements for their personnel. The inadequate flexibility of such rules of deployment meant that they turned out to be excessively restrictive when it came to the Helmand theatre, preventing civilians from providing the necessary degree of developmental and political support to the military effort.[52] Once again, this reflected the lack of institutional insight (and foresight) that characterised the planning stage of the Helmand campaign, resulting in a failure to anticipate how uniquely challenging the mission would be and to adjust existing arrangements accordingly.

The 2005 Joint Plan represented a genuine attempt to operationalise the UK's comprehensive approach, but was perhaps destined to have a much more limited impact in 2006 than originally hoped. Some officials have even suggested that

---

[50] HCDC, *The Comprehensive Approach*, *op. cit.*, p. 19.

[51] Author interview with former MoD official, September 2011.

[52] HCDC, *The Comprehensive Approach*, *op. cit.*, p. 36.

the UK should not have had a 'national' plan for Helmand insofar as the country was meant to be part of an international campaign.[53] The original NATO strategy aimed to establish mechanisms of good governance in the whole of Afghanistan; essential to this was the provision of adequate levels of security. Yet the Alliance's plan was too broad and general,[54] and therefore failed to provide sufficiently specific guidelines that could have helped its members better co-ordinate their regional initiatives. Most importantly, it lacked a strong, unifying figure that could lead the whole effort politically and represent the point of reference for the military. From a British perspective, there was very little interaction with the NATO or Canadian plan, which would have made it possible to achieve at least a more harmonised approach in the south of the country.[55] Instead, the prevailing state of mind in London was that the Helmand campaign was going to be a national, unilateral endeavour.

Ultimately, though, the plan was unworkable for the kind of environment Helmand presented at the time. The strategic assumptions upon which it was originally based were to change the very moment British troops deployed in the region. From this perspective, the subsequent move to the north only accelerated the deterioration of already-volatile security conditions; it did not invalidate, in itself, the Joint Plan. Even if kept limited to the 'lozenge', it was far from certain that such a plan could have been delivered without suffering significant disruption as a consequence of the Taliban offensive that would probably have reached Lashkar Gah and Gereshk,[56] had not it been blunted by the UK's own kinetic initiative of summer 2006.

---

[53] Author interview with former MoD official, September 2011. The point remains hotly contested and it is worth pointing out that a number of substantial improvements were made subsequently, including the posting of stabilisation advisers into districts.

[54] Author interview with former MoD official, September 2011.

[55] Author interview with former MoD official, September 2011.

[56] Evidence by Peter Wall to the HCDC, *Operations in Afghanistan*, *op. cit.*, Ev. 146.

Conclusion

In 2005, the UK's Afghan campaign was still overshadowed by the concurrent effort in Iraq. The fact that the country was continuing to struggle in the latter theatre made it extremely hard for practitioners on the ground and politicians in Whitehall to learn quickly enough to prevent the same flawed approach from later being adopted in Helmand. The willingness to view the Helmand mission as an opportunity to offset what had gone wrong in Iraq led to unrealistic ambitions, especially considering that the level of intellectual resources committed to the effort was not capable of turning them into reality.

Albeit valid conceptually, the UK's comprehensive approach lacked reliable and solid foundations that should have been provided by a sound strategic policy planning process, in turn enhanced by a genuinely cross-government engagement. Instead, the compartmentalised attitude which still prevailed led to a weak and tentative commitment to the envisaged strategy from the very stakeholders who were supposed to champion and promote it.

Since 2006, there have been substantial and remarkable improvements in the UK's strategic approach to the Helmand campaign. These have translated into a more coherent, and genuinely joint, mission plan. The 2008 Helmand Road Map and the 2010 Helmand Implementation Plan represent a manifestation of a progressive adjustment, which has allowed an effective realignment of ends, ways and means. Many of the fundamental weaknesses that negatively impacted on the 2005 Joint Plan have been successfully addressed; first and foremost, the compartmentalised structure of the planning process and the split between the planning and the delivery teams on the ground. When 52 Brigade took over command of the province in 2007, it interacted extensively with the PCRU in an effort to recalibrate the UK's overall strategy by suggesting more realistic objectives,[57] determining a more appropriate level of resources to devote to the campaign and better co-ordinating military and civilian lines of activity to achieve the ultimate strategic aims. This bottom-up approach has proved to be much more conducive to the

---

[57] Farrell and Gordon, *op. cit.*, p. 21.

achievement of a truly integrated campaign plan, demonstrating the UK's serious commitment to the comprehensive approach.

However, it may be too soon to tell whether a solid process of institutional learning is now in place; both the experience of the Balkans and Iraq had previously provided the opportunity to develop a proper understanding of the peculiar challenges associated with nation-building. This should have prompted a continuous refinement of institutional memory. In fact, the UK failed in this effort because it was unable to establish an appropriate mechanism for learning and incorporating such valuable lessons. In Afghanistan, as rightly pointed out by Butler, the country therefore had to re-learn those lessons, painfully and expensively,[58] before finally getting the approach right.

There is reason to believe that, as dramatic as it was, the 2006 Helmand campaign might have succeeded in focusing minds – in Whitehall and across the whole of the UK's strategy-making establishment – on the need to be genuinely and coherently 'joined-up' in the approach to modern conflict. But such genuine commitment must not be lost on the way towards the next big engagement and should instead be further enhanced. Cross-departmental interaction should become a seamless mechanism to promote real integration.

Finally, the complexities attached to nation-building, highlighted once more by the Helmand mission, seem to suggest the need for a more discretionary approach to intervention in the future. Today, military victory is only one part of a much wider and longer commitment, which, in the reconstruction phase, poses the greatest challenge. In an era of major budget cuts, the UK will have to consider more carefully where, when and, most crucially, how to play a significant role. It can no longer be taken for granted that the resources necessary to embark on a prolonged mission will be there, let alone that the country will be able to sustain two concurrent campaigns of this kind in the future. The short-sighted attitude which allowed this to happen in Afghanistan and Iraq has been averted in the case of

---

[58] Evidence by Ed Butler to the HCDC, *The Comprehensive Approach*, *op. cit.*, Ev. 15.

the Libyan intervention, where the option of putting UK troops on the ground was never regarded as a viable one. The process of institutional learning necessary to refine the British way of strategy-making may finally be on track.

CANADA IN REGIONAL COMMAND SOUTH: ALLIANCE DYNAMICS AND NATIONAL IMPERATIVES

MATTHEW WILLIS

Canada's involvement in Afghanistan has lasted a decade, from the late-2001 deployment of its special forces, sent to exterminate Al-Qa'ida in the south of the country, to the training mission Canadian troops began this summer in Kabul. In between, Ottawa deployed the Canadian Forces once to Kabul and twice to Kandahar. The second southern mission, begun in 2005, became the fullest and costliest mobilisation of men and materiel Canada had undertaken since the Korean War. Though Canada never fielded as many personnel as its American or major European counterparts, the highest figure being somewhere just shy of 3,000, its military was well-trained, well-equipped and largely free of obstructive caveats and restrictive rules of engagement.[1] Initial qualms that the Canadian Forces had lost their ability to do combat had been dispelled by their first deployment in Kandahar in 2002 (something the public absorbed with a mix of chagrin and pride) and when Britain deployed on its fateful mission to Helmand in 2006, it did so with Canada in Kandahar on its eastern flank.

Canada's deployment quickly became controversial for its unanticipated cost in blood and treasure, and for the lack of

[1] Initial deployments had been subject to tighter rules.

progress on what was ostensibly its primary purpose: reconstruction. As in Britain – and to a lesser extent the Netherlands, which shared command responsibilities for Regional Command (RC) South with the UK and Canada – the policy process leading to the mission came under scrutiny. The competence of the political leadership and motives of the planners – particularly the defence department and the military – were viewed with particular suspicion.

Canada's participation in Stage 3 has been studied extensively from a national angle, and is rightly seen as a watershed in the way Canada engaged with the world. Among other things, it underscored the post-9/11 take on the linkage between international and national security, shattered deep-seated popular – as well as official – notions as to the purpose of the military instrument, and injected new dynamism into the debate surrounding civil-military relations in Canada. But Kandahar was not just a Canadian mission. It had significant international dimensions, in relation both to NATO's overall strategy for Afghanistan and the Alliance's campaign in the southern provinces. Most fundamentally, perhaps, to a British reader, Kandahar helped 'make' Helmand: had not Ottawa insisted that the Canadian Forces deploy where they did, British soldiers would have spent the last half-decade not in Helmand, but in the next province along.

The Canadian deployment to Kandahar is best understood as a function of three inter-related drivers.

First, the Afghan strategic context. Frequently overlooked, NATO's plan for ISAF's phased expansion beyond Kabul was an extremely powerful conditioner of national policy processes.[2] Not only did it entail advance commitment from Ottawa, virtually locking it into future contributions, but membership in the Alliance brought with it obligations that could not be ignored.

[2] The NATO plan was above all political, agreed in the North Atlantic Council, which means treating it as a force fully separate from – and thus acting *on* – national governments is not strictly correct. Having agreed to the strategy, however, Ottawa, London and the rest did commit themselves to it, for which reason it will be treated here as a force exerting pressure on them.

Second, Canada's own preferences. Experience gained in Kandahar in 2002 and Kabul in 2003, but particularly in the Yugoslav Wars of the 1990s, strongly influenced the Canadian attitude towards any kind of deployment – what was acceptable and what was not, and what the pay-off needed to be to make a mission worthwhile.

Third, the UK's decision to deploy to the south. Britain's deployment was a prerequisite for any Canadian mission to the region. It made Kandahar possible. The early date at which Canada began exploring the possibility of going south – well ahead of NATO's timeline, but contemporary with similar thinking in London, underscores the Anglo-Canadian connection at a time US attention was focused elsewhere.

A National Outlook Shaped by Strategic-Level Forces

NATO took over ISAF in August 2003. Canada and Germany were among the take-over's prime proponents. For countries wishing to see ISAF expand beyond the capital region, NATO's leadership made participation politically palatable, which it would not have been under American leadership.[3] This was a central German interest. It also reassured countries that were, in principle, willing to commit troops that replacement nations would be found for them.[4] That was a Canadian concern. The United States, which had been exerting pressure on its fellow Alliance members to take on more of the burden of the mission, was supportive of the idea too, despite initial reluctance. Critically, this move laid the foundations of Canada's mission to Kandahar: the plan that accompanied it, for ISAF's phased, counter-clockwise expansion into the four corners of Afghanistan, entailed advance commitments from member nations. Canada's defence minister, John McCallum, pledged a PRT at the Brussels NATO summit in December 2003.[5]

---

[3] Rick Hillier, *A Soldier First: Bullets, Bureaucrats and the Politics of War* (Toronto: HarperCollins, 2009), p. 281.

[4] *Ibid.*; see also Janice Gross-Stein and Eugene Lang, *The Unexpected War: Canada in Kandahar* (Toronto: Viking Canada, 2007), pp. 66, 95–96.

[5] Stein and Lang, *op. cit.*, pp. 132–33.

Kabul was the main focus in Ottawa in the early weeks of 2004. Third Battalion, Royal Canadian Regiment, had been deployed there since August 2003, and General Rick Hillier, Chief of the Land Staff, was due to assume command of ISAF in February for the second half of Canada's one-year commitment. Some have suggested that Kabul – a relatively low-risk mission – was seen by the political and military leadership as a convenient way for Canada to begin extricating itself from Afghanistan, a process the even-safer PRT mission would round out.[6] But those closely involved in planning contradict this theory, saying it was well understood that Kabul in fact marked the start of a multi-year engagement for Canada. Kenneth Calder, the assistant deputy minister in the Department of National Defence (DND) then responsible for policy, observes that no one 'had any illusions about this being over quickly.'[7] Indeed, the writing had been on the wall for months: though McCallum had pledged the PRT in December 2003, the planning behind it had begun immediately following NATO's take-over of ISAF. By January, the only question was when, where and how big the next deployment would be.

That had yet to be determined – it was still too early and Kabul was soaking up everyone's energy – but anyone who could read the signs knew roughly where and when it must take place. General Ray Henault, Canada's chief of the Defence Staff, had already decreed that following Kabul, the Canadian Forces would require eighteen months to rest, train and re-equip – an operational pause, in other words.[8] The odds of Canada partaking in ISAF's Stage 2 expansion, scheduled to begin in

---

[6] *Ibid.*, p. 108.

[7] Author interview with Ken Calder, 23 June 2011. John McCallum, then-defence minister, has also stated that Ottawa was not averse to a post-Kabul redeployment. The one thing the government demanded, however, was that commitments be made one at a time, for agreed durations, and that the Canadian Forces be relieved on schedule. Author interview with John McCallum, 5 August 2011.

[8] Henault made the decision in 2003.

mid-2005, were thus slim. By the same token, a deployment as part of Stages 3 or 4 – to the south or east – was much more likely.[9]

Canada was just one of many countries pondering its next deployment, and among them was the Netherlands, where similar calculations were being made. The Dutch knew that ISAF's expansion would mean volunteering to take on an Afghan province, just as the Canadians did, and as early as March 2004, the subject arose between them bilaterally.[10] The Dutch were keen to know what the Canadians were thinking.

As it became clear that spring that the UK's calls to rationalise the US's Operation *Enduring Freedom* and NATO's ISAF were going to bear fruit, resulting in the latter's incorporation of some of the former's higher-end objectives, Dutch and Canadian thinking was focused further. In the relatively calm provinces, the addition of security responsibilities to reconstruction efforts would matter little; but in the restive southern ones, it was likely to mean far tougher deployments. A quick look at the NATO 'league tables' – the unofficial record every country kept of what every other country was doing (or not doing) – and it was plain that not many governments would volunteer for a southern mission. For two nations with proud military traditions, capable forces and a strong commitment to the Alliance, the implications were stark.

Canadian Preferences

Before Canada determined it would mount a mission in southern Afghanistan, it examined two other options: Chaghcharan and Herat, both in the west. These were regions to which NATO, and specifically General Jim Jones, Supreme Allied Commander Europe (SACEUR), were keen for Canada to deploy. In the end, for a range of reasons relating to Canadian national preferences, neither was deemed suitable. The preferences

---

[9] The allegation that it was bureaucratic bickering and indecisiveness that determined the timing and location of Canada's eventual deployment, as opposed to the Canadian Forces force-generation timeline, is spurious.

[10] Author interview with Vice Admiral Drew Robertson, 10 October 2011.

themselves are generally well-known, but their underpinnings are not.

In the former Yugoslavia, Canada had made a significant contribution to international missions, beginning with UNPROFOR in 1992, but had not gained proportional recognition or influence over political or military strategic decisions. The main reason was that its units had been assigned to larger formations under the command of other countries, and it was those countries, who had gained the visibility that command brought, that had had recognition and influence. Besides limiting Canada's visibility, the geographic separation of its units had made the overall effort less sustainable and more costly.[11] In November 1999, Canada decided to rationalise its contribution to the former Yugoslavia in both the NATO-led Stabilisation Force (SFOR) in Bosnia and Herzegovina and Kosovo Force (KFOR) by concentrating the bulk of its resources on a larger commitment in SFOR. In doing so it not only improved the sustainability of its deployed forces, but also gained recognition for its shared role in the rotating command of Multinational Division (later Brigade) Southwest, in partnership with the Netherlands and Britain.[12]

The influence of the Balkan experience on Canadian thinking in 2004 – a short five years later – cannot be overstated. Concentration of force and demonstrability of impact became all-important considerations in planning circles. Any mission that did not permit the first or lend itself to the second would be viewed particularly unfavourably. The reason went well beyond a Canadian desire to be patted on the back. It was about being able to make one's voice heard in the political and military fora where mission-defining decisions were being taken, including, not least, plans for the use of Canadian soldiers. It was thus also about improving Canada's ability to exert its influence in accordance with its interests and values.

Neither Chaghcharan nor Herat lent itself to achieving Canadian aims. Chaghcharan was a backwater, where Canada's

---

[11] Author interview with Vice Admiral Robertson, 10 October 2011. For an additional Canadian view, see Hillier, *op. cit.*, pp. 155–58.

[12] The Canadian commander was Major General Rick Hillier.

contribution would have had little strategic impact and even less visibility. Chaghcharan also lacked crucial infrastructure, including a suitable airfield, which would have aggravated the logistical challenges and danger involved in any deployment.[13] Herat had drawbacks, too: beyond its being of secondary strategic importance, going there would have meant a shared command with Italy, which no one in Ottawa was keen on. Moreover, the Italians could manage without Canadian help; the Canadian Forces contribution would be more worthwhile elsewhere.

Much of the Canadian leadership's aversion to partnering with the Italians or certain other European nations had to do with another pre-existing preference, in which the experience of former Yugoslavia also figured. A second lesson the military had learnt in Bosnia was that there were real advantages to working with partners, but particularly 'like-minded' partners: ones with similar military capabilities, political and military outlook, ways of operating and general ethos. NATO membership encouraged a degree of homogenisation in some of these areas, but not nearly enough, which officials in the Canadian military had had ample opportunity to appreciate over the course of the 2002 and 2003 deployments in Kandahar and Kabul. Canada's experience in Multinational Division Southwest in Bosnia, on the other hand, had left the military leadership with a very favourable view of Britain and the Netherlands, translating into a degree of comfort with them that only further dampened enthusiasm for other partnerships. On the basis of their MND Southwest collaboration, the British and Dutch had similarly positive views of each other and the Canadians.[14] The desire for

[13] The prospect of being within another country's sphere of influence – the Italians were going to be running the PRT in neighbouring Herat – has also been cited as a concern. For the views of Bill Graham and General Henault, see Stein and Lang, *op. cit.*, pp. 135–37.

[14] Indeed, a senior Dutch source observed that the Dutch military considered NATO planning processes inadequate for the complicated southern region, and was therefore keen to develop operational procedures with partners it could trust – like Canada and Britain. Private correspondence with former Dutch Ministry of Defence official, 22 September 2011.

partnership with like-minded nations was independent of any geopolitical preferences, but did create a predisposition towards exploring mission options favouring the 'right' sort of collaboration, should any crop up.

There was no point at which thinking about the 'mission-that-became-Kandahar' formally began. Nonetheless, if for convenience's sake it can be said there came a point at which the idea of a 'post-Kabul mission' began taking on substance, Canadian preferences had without doubt already structured thinking on what it would be like. Taken together, those preferences amounted to a fairly coherent policy line: Canada was going to make a single, prolonged, whole-of-government contribution that brought the best out of its military and civilian agencies, and it was going to do so with like-minded partners if possible. By implication, while there was no preconceived idea as to *where* the Canadian Forces might wind up, there was a very clear vision as to what a deployment must *involve* if Ottawa were to commit to it. These expectations, in turn, implied certain things about the type of province that would be suitable for a Canadian mission. The Balkan imprint on Canadian thinking here is unmistakable.

The United Kingdom

Britain had been instrumental in shaping the strategic NATO context since 2003. Alarmed at indications the Alliance was running out of steam – General Sir Rob Fry at one point described the campaign as 'moribund'[15] – it had followed up its push for ISAF leadership via the Allied Rapid Reaction Corps by advocating for the rationalising of Operation *Enduring Freedom* and ISAF.[16] UK actions had sent Canadian planners strong signals.

---

[15] House of Commons Defence Committee [HCDC], *Operations in Afghanistan*, Fourth Report of Session 2010–12, HC 554 (London: The Stationery Office, July 2011), Ev. 397.

[16] Bringing some kind of coherence to the West's two-pronged campaign was in fact a precondition of the UK's leadership of ISAF.

The move to assume leadership of ISAF, meanwhile, had strongly implied the beefing-up of the UK's military presence[17] and the date at which it would occur.

The streamlining of *Enduring Freedom* and ISAF, as discussed, had all but guaranteed the southern provinces would be available for anyone with the guts to call them. It was therefore no surprise that in mid-2004 (possibly earlier) Ottawa received confirmation that the UK was indeed planning to shift south in a major way.[18] A potential deployment to the south in early 2006 was now not only plausible from a force-generation standpoint and logical in view of Canadian 'mission preferences', it was also – for the first time – logistically practicable: substantial though it was, the US presence at Kandahar Airfield alone would not have been sufficient to make a Canadian mission in the region feasible.[19]

It was around this time that SACEUR began to solicit Canada's presence in the west as he struggled to fill Stage 2 PRT slots. Throughout the summer and autumn, he made overtures to Canada to assume responsibility first for Chaghcharan, then Herat. General Henault travelled to both in the summer of 2004 and a number of other visits by various Canadian officials followed. Despite continued pressure from General Jones into the autumn, however, Henault resisted: the UK and Canada had begun serious talks about deploying together to the south, and they were going well.

---

[17] See testimony by Lord Reid before the HCDC, *Operations in Afghanistan, op. cit.*, Ev. 401.

[18] Author interviews with Ken Calder, 23 June 2011, and General Henault, 1 September 2011. British Chief of the Defence Staff, Sir Michael Walker, who was close to General Henault and had visited him in Ottawa in January 2004, may well have given Henault a heads-up then.

[19] Author interviews with Ken Calder, 5 September 2011, and General Henault, 1 September 2011. Henault was firm on this point, saying that without a 'good, solid partnership' with a 'like-minded' country – meaning the UK – Canada would not have been able to do the Kandahar mission.

Establishing a precise timeline of the discussions may never be possible, owing to their frequently informal basis and the dearth of written records kept.[20] What is certain, however, is that by the time David Reddaway, the British high commissioner, voiced the UK's interest in partnering with Canada in the Kandahar region to Canada's foreign minister, Bill Graham, in October, lower-level talks between London and Ottawa had been underway for some time. In his memoirs, General Hillier provides clear substantiation as to the timeframe. 'Even before I returned from commanding ISAF', he writes, 'NATO had announced its intentions to expand the ISAF mission beyond Kabul in 2006, and planning was already well on its way for a move into Kandahar Province by the time I landed back in Canada that fall.' Hillier returned from Afghanistan in late September 2004.[21]

The bilateral dynamic reportedly took SACEUR by surprise. Relating the difficulties NATO planners had been having pulling together contributions for western Afghanistan, a source close to SACEUR recalled how, in response to Jones's persistent requests for a contribution, Canada volunteered 'more or less out of the blue' – as it seemed – to take on Kandahar. The offer to fill a slot in what would have been Stage 3 was welcome, came the response, but was not relevant to the task at hand and so could not be endorsed at that time. The Canadians were unfazed. 'The Canadians and the British,' said

[20] Indeed, even DND and Canadian Forces officials intimately involved in the planning process often have little more than a notional sense of timing (or do not feel able to be more precise), something equally common in the UK and Netherlands.

[21] Hillier, *op. cit.*, p. 342. He reiterates the point on the following page, saying the 'government had already signaled its intent to go into Kandahar Province, and the Department of Foreign Affairs, CIDA and National Defence *were well into their planning* of that mission by the time I came back to work at NDHQ after my time as ISAF commander [emphasis added]' (p. 343). Calder also asserted that by the time the Chaghcharan suggestion surfaced, and thus even before Herat, the defence department was already 'going to Kandahar as far as they were concerned.' Author interview, 5 September 2011.

the source, 'hammered out the whole thing without NATO's assistance, behind closed doors. ... We were not aware of the details.'[22]

General Jones was typically well-informed as to the plans and thinking of NATO countries' military leaders, so it may seem surprising to some – unlikely, even – that he should not have anticipated the Canadian offer. One must bear in mind, however, the high degree of secrecy necessarily surrounding partnership discussions (particularly informal ones) owing to their political sensitivity. Considerable groundwork needed to be laid on both the Canadian and British sides before anyone was prepared to speak about a partnership, and those proceedings would have been conducted with utmost discretion.

Kandahar

Why Canada ended up in Kandahar and Britain in Helmand remains something of a mystery. Intriguingly, the testimony of British generals indicates that the UK had originally planned to go to Kandahar itself, the feeling having been that the most powerful nation should take the keystone province.[23] The British appear to have ceded Kandahar only when their counterparts made it clear that Canadian participation in the mission hinged on going there. General Fry, speaking before the House of Commons Defence Committee, seemed to suggest that, in part, the UK was willing to back down because it could justify deploying to Helmand just as easily as Kandahar.[24]

It is also possible, though, that UK timelines and subtle US pressure played into the decision. It had been agreed by this

---

[22] Which is not to say this taking of initiative was viewed as problematic. 'More power to them' was SACEUR's view. Author interview with a former assistant to SACEUR, 11 August 2011.

[23] General David Richards outlines his thinking in James Fergusson, *A Million Bullets: The Real Story of the British Army in Afghanistan* (London: Bantam, 2008), pp. 232–33. Incidentally, the Dutch had also been eyeing Kandahar, abandoning the idea only when they learned it had already gone to Canada.

[24] HCDC, *Operations in Afghanistan*, *op. cit.*, Ev. 409.

point that Operation *Enduring Freedom* and ISAF would be streamlined and that operations in the south would fall under NATO command. This suited the US, which was eager to get the southern provinces off its hands, even though it had committed to furnishing the troops required for Stage 4 (under NATO) later on. But key to handing off the south was having someone to take the baton.

Although General Henault's operational pause was still due to last till December, resources would be available to be shifted southwards from Kabul beginning in July, and Canada's base in the capital would be dismantled throughout the autumn. Canadian forces thus had the capacity to handle relatively light PRT responsibilities and the co-ordination involved in the *Enduring Freedom*-to-ISAF transition. Henault has indeed remarked that a final reason for Canada's going to Kandahar was to provide a reliable 'anchor tenant' for the ISAF mission.[25] The end of Canada's mission in Kabul therefore meant it was better positioned than the UK to get boots on the ground early. Britain was still tied up in Mazar-e-Sharif and Kabul – and perhaps most importantly of all, in Iraq. Indeed, it was the projected pace of Britain's draw-down in Basra that appears to have dictated the rate of its ramp-up in Afghanistan from the start, and that could hardly be sped up. Canada's flexibility, combined with the UK's own commitments, could well have earned the Canadian planners the backing of the US in their negotiations with the British.[26]

Whatever the reasons, the negotiations between the Canadians and British on respective locations had come to an end by December 2004. On 9 December, at the NATO foreign ministers meeting, Pierre Pettigrew announced that Canada would be establishing a PRT in Kandahar. That announcement would not have been made unless talks had progressed far enough to warrant the Canadian Cabinet being brought into the picture prior to the

[25] Author interview with General Henault, 21 July 2011.

[26] A Dutch defence official close to the planning of the southern deployment has also suggested that the Canadians believed Helmand would require more troops than they were willing, or perhaps able, to deploy.

conference. Additional details of the mission, beyond the mere location, were agreed informally on the margins of the February 2005 Munich Security Conference.[27]

The Netherlands was also on board by late 2004. From the moment it had been decided NATO would expand ISAF counter-clockwise, the Dutch had known they would be expected to contribute. According to a senior Dutch defence official, the signs were not difficult to read. Member state preferences were obvious, and the least desirable regions were always going to be in the south and east. As one of the few players with adequate military capacity, the Netherlands knew what NATO would expect of it. Duty was not the only consideration, of course. The Dutch had some of the same logistical requirements as the Canadians, specifically an airfield. Because Canada had succeeded in securing Kandahar, which the Dutch had been eyeing themselves for a time, Uruzgan emerged as the next-most-suitable place.[28] It is safe to suggest that the ultimate choice of Uruzgan was the product of both the forces of circumstance, as in the Canadian case, and Dutch preferences which emerged over time.

Obtaining prime ministerial approval was the next step. The crucial meeting took place on 21 March 2005, attended by then-Prime Minister Paul Martin and his close advisors, General Hillier (who had recently succeeded General Henault as Chief of the Defence Staff), and senior officials from the defence and foreign ministries. Martin, after securing a guarantee from Hillier that a mission to Kandahar would not preclude future deployments to other hot spots, pronounced himself amenable

[27] Author interview with Ken Calder, 23 June 2011.

[28] All of the above based on private correspondence with a former Dutch Ministry of Defence official, 22 September 2011. The Dutch did not appear to be aware of the bilateral Canada-UK dynamic when they began exploring options concretely in late 2004. They approached the British about joining forces in the hopes that being proactive would reduce the odds of their being forced to accept a deployment location later on (dictated by NATO) that suited them less well. That the Canadians and British were already well into talks underscores just how early their planning process had begun.

to the plan and agreed to consider three deployment packages. Over the months that followed, a Cabinet committee reviewed the proposed configurations and chose the one Canada would supply, after which the full Cabinet formally approved the deployment. In May, the government made public the decision to take on the Kandahar mission.

Domestic Controversy

Although Kandahar has come to be called 'Harper's war' – in reference to current Prime Minister Stephen Harper, who succeeded Martin and extended Canada's commitment twice – the bulk of the controversy has surrounded the decisions taken under his predecessor. Owing to the enduring popular attachment to Canada's (largely mythical) peacekeeping tradition, Kandahar is widely construed as a radical departure from the pattern established by the original Kandahar and Kabul deployments. The meeting at which Martin was persuaded to approve the deployment is portrayed as the point at which Canadian soldiers were sent 'from the relative comfort of Kabul to the pointy edge of combat in the turbulent south.'[29] Certainly, owing to the beefing-up of the ISAF mandate and the mission's geography, it was known that the 2005–06 deployment was liable to be noticeably more intense than the Kabul mission. To say that defence planners and the politicians believed they were committing the Canadian Forces to a combat mission, however, is to distort the facts. Paul Martin clearly states that although he understood the troops would be engaged in 'peace-making' rather than peacekeeping activities,[30] '[I]n my time as prime minister, we never envisaged a broad military campaign that would make reconstruction efforts more difficult if not impossible.'[31]

---

[29] See Bill Schiller, 'The Road to Kandahar', *Toronto Star*, 9 September 2006.
[30] Paul Martin, *Hell or High Water: My Life In and Out of Politics* (Toronto: McClelland and Stewart, 2009), p. 392.
[31] *Ibid.*, p. 395.

Calder, Henault and others have said the same thing: everyone knew the mission would be tough, but no one anticipated how strong the Taliban would become. The American presence in the region had been so light to that point that little intelligence was available on Taliban strength or intentions, but the US troops had not been unduly molested.[32] Both the British and Dutch militaries were – on the whole – comfortable with the mission (it was the Dutch politicians, not the generals, who had qualms) and the senior UK leadership, like the Canadian, has been emphatic that nobody expected they were about to disturb a hornets' nest. In 2004 and 2005, when strategic decisions were being made, Kandahar was not meant to be the kind of mission it became.

The failure to anticipate the number, ferocity and resilience of the 'hornets' is a second key area of controversy, much of it boiling down to the (non-)availability of intelligence and its analysis. This matter, largely the same in Canada as in Britain, has been treated elsewhere; but it invites the equally contentious question why the senior Canadian military leadership, and the defence and foreign affairs departments, persisted in pushing the mission forward. Ostensibly, the military was seeking redemption after a decade of unremarkable performances in unremarkable (read: peacekeeping) theatres; or perhaps it wanted to show the US, the Canadian public and other key allies that it really could do combat if called on. The supposed enthusiasm of the foreign affairs department for doing something 'dramatic' – ignored by commentators until recently – is another theory.[33] Implicit and

---

[32] It has recently been suggested that US special forces in Kandahar had known, or at least strongly suspected, that the Taliban were 'playing possum', deliberately lulling the Canadians, British and Dutch into a false sense of security in order then to hit them even harder when they arrived. It may be some time before the veracity of the claim can be tested. See Brian Stewart, 'Canada in Kandahar, Wrong Place, Wrong Time', *CBC News*, 9 June 2011.

[33] *Ibid.*

sometimes explicit in all of the above is the idea that Canadian planners were pursuing a principally national agenda divorced from the NATO plan and heavily conditioned by beliefs about what would go over well in Washington.[34] A putative disconnect between the civil and military bureaucracies – which presented Kandahar as a *fait accompli*, and the government – wary of the mission but eventually cajoled into it, is also at the heart of these narratives.

Without doubt, the impulse to 'go big or go home' was present on the side of the planners and military, and it is equally clear that Canada – and the UK and Netherlands – were operating quasi-independently of NATO. After all, they had virtually hammered out what would become the core of ISAF's Phase 3 before SACEUR had even firmed up Stage 2. But the picture is not black and white. For one, at this stage NATO still had not put its stamp on the mission to the extent it later would; there was still an expectation that member nations would take some form of initiative. Second, the senior military leadership was not as gung-ho about Afghanistan as it is made out to have been. In 2002, General Henault had had to refuse a request by the defence minister to extend Canada's one-rotation deployment to Kandahar. In 2003, it was General Hillier's turn to inform another defence minister that the army could not manage more than a one-year mission to Kabul. And it was Henault, again in 2003, who decided that the Canadian Forces would need an operational pause once Kabul was over. On the whole, Canada's generals were cautious about taking on more than the country could handle.

Moreover, once the mission was in the works, it was better not to back into it. General Hillier has been wrongly portrayed as the architect of the Kandahar mission and the one who increased the size and capacity of the Canadian contingent, most notably insisting that Canada must have a headquarters and thus

[34] A variant on this view is that defence planners were actually pursuing a *defence* agenda divorced from national interests, where DND/Canadian Forces objectives were heavily conditioned by US military preferences.

command capability when it deployed.[35] His insistence on going 'whole hog' has been cast as hubris, and no one who came into contact with him would deny he was strongly in favour of the mission. But Hillier had witnessed first-hand the embarrassments of Bosnia as well as the problems flowing from under-capable ISAF contingents during his spell in Kabul; he was also among Canada's most experienced field commanders. Having, in a sense, inherited Kandahar, he had to make sure the Canadian force was as prepared as it could be, and that meant not sending it in under-manned and under-equipped. Certainly in hindsight, no one can argue the contingent he saw deployed was too robust.

Such debates notwithstanding, what does seem clear is that tougher questions should have been asked on the Canadian side about the country's ability to generate enough manpower and materiel. Even if a force of 2,300 was a not-unreasonable initial deployment (bearing in mind the UK started off with just over 3,100), planners could not have been blind to the fact that they were already sending close to the maximum number of soldiers available into theatre. There was little capacity for a ramp-up, and generals who knew they were entering *terra incognita* should have been concerned about that vulnerability.

Conclusion

There can be no doubt both Kandahar and Helmand were flawed missions. Attempts to understand them, however, must take account of the difference between the strategic and operational levels. Which country went to which province was the product of mainly strategic-level decision-making; what capabilities were deployed and how they were used were separate, operational questions, and the planning that settled them was carried out later. This chapter's purpose was to shed light on policy drivers at the Canadian strategic level and to examine the overlap between

---

[35] For portrayals of Hillier, see, for example, Stein and Lang, *op. cit.*, or Kimberly Marten, 'From Kabul to Kandahar: The Canadian Forces and Change,' *American Review of Canadian Studies* (Vol. 40, No. 2, June 2010), pp. 214–36.

planning for Kandahar and Helmand at that same level. It was not meant, therefore, to assess whether or not Kandahar was run as well as it might have been in theatre, nor does it attempt to.

Canada's deployment to Kandahar was the outcome of a diffuse and organic policy process that was driven by events at least as much as it was led by Canadian planners. The major policy determinants can be divided into three sets. First, Kandahar was made plausible and even logical by strategic-level developments triggered by political decisions in NATO. Those decisions, some of which Canada had supported and even instigated, played an integral part in conditioning the country's future policy options. Second, Canadian mission preferences, shaped to a significant extent by Canada's experience in the former Yugoslavia as well as by its prior Afghan deployments, rendered some missions inherently more or less appealing. Those preferences coalesced into what amounted to a policy line demanding a single, substantial and sustained whole-of-government effort; a mission involving partnerships with like-minded nations; and a commitment that would bring the best out of Canada's military. Finally, Britain's decision to deploy into the south was not merely a precondition of any Canadian southern mission: it was what tipped the scales decisively in favour of one. The early date at which Canada and the UK began discussing a Stage 3 deployment, far in advance of NATO's timeline but nonetheless driven by it, attests to the strength of the link between the countries.

Of these policy drivers, the most remarkable is undoubtedly the strength of NATO's own dynamics. By virtue of the government-level commitments extracted in fora like the North Atlantic Council, political decisions taken in NATO exerted far-reaching influence. This observation invites several more. First, Canada was likely not the only country to have found its policy options shaped by the Alliance's strategy, and it would be interesting to study the decision-making processes of other medium and small contributors with this in mind. Second, though some might view NATO's influence over policy at the national level with unease, it is probably actually a sign that the Alliance was working as it was meant to. Third, there is an obvious caveat to points one and two: they only hold if a sense of duty to the Alliance, such as that exhibited by Canada, the Netherlands and the UK, features in Alliance members' defence and foreign policies, and thus their governments.

None of which is to suggest that planners and decision-makers in Ottawa were robbed of agency and under inexorable pressure to undertake a southern deployment. They were not. Someone, sometime, could have halted the process. Nonetheless, the view – expressed at senior levels in Ottawa, London and The Hague alike – that there was a feeling of inevitability surrounding what became the Stage 3 deployments should not be dismissed. Unpalatable though it might seem, Canada's deployment to Regional Command South may very simply have been an ill-starred mission that then went wrong. In Afghanistan, stranger things have happened.

UK NATIONAL STRATEGY AND HELMAND

ROBERT FRY AND
DESMOND BOWEN

The UK policy response to the 9/11 attacks was immediate and categorical: the ungoverned space of Afghanistan must be denied to Al-Qa'ida as a haven and prospective base for mounting future operations. This position gained formal and general expression with the publication in 2002 of the New Chapter addendum to the Strategic Defence Review of 1998. The New Chapter made clear that, in the British view, terrorism at home had to be addressed by forward defence in Central Asia or wherever the contingent threat emanated from. This view can be, and was latterly, criticised as supine conformity to US policy and an approach informed by the vacuous idea of a global war on terrorism: a war against a condition and therefore, by definition, unwinnable and with few pointers to the appropriate application of the instruments of national power. Nonetheless, the policy requirement at the outset was clear and the challenge then became to create a strategy to deliver it; or, alternatively stated, how to reconcile political ends with military (and other) means.

The UK's coincidence of strategic purpose with the US stemmed from a deep-rooted sense of security being indivisible in the face of a potent transnational threat. There was also recognition that Afghanistan had been left to stew in its own juice after the Soviet withdrawal – indeed, positively neglected – and the result had been civil war, Taliban government and Al-Qa'ida basing. NATO's invocation of Article V of its founding treaty provided a broader context for the sense of collective threat and an inalienable responsibility to respond. This combination of factors led, initially, to the deployment of forces under national command which were subsequently brought under NATO auspices. It is arguable that the rapid defeat of the Taliban regime in 2001 deprived Al-Qa'ida of its client sponsor and so achieved the strategic end. That was not the view taken at the time, either nationally or within the UN Security Council; on the contrary, it was judged that any enduring solution must be underwritten by effective governance of a unitary Afghan state from Kabul. In other words, that the end-state required a political solution and not merely the effective application of military force.

This view was given clear expression at the Bonn Conference which ushered in a wider political process involving an interim Afghan government and the negotiation of a new constitution, followed by phased elections, and all underwritten by the UN. In parallel, Provincial Reconstruction Teams (PRTs) were conceived and their deployment initiated on an exploratory basis in the north of Afghanistan, first under national command and later under NATO. The device of the PRT was created as an economy of force solution to extending the reach of government, its funds and the potential for social and economic development by providing a protected platform for civil agencies. The NATO plan included a British PRT in Mazar-e-Sharif, which provided a broadly successful model for development elsewhere, though there was no single, universal template.

As the plan rolled out, the northern half of Afghanistan entered into a broadly compliant relationship with NATO forces and the Karzai government. The operation was not without its flaws, amongst which the role of atavistic warlordism and the associated limitations of central governance were prominent. And, at the level of theatre command, the bifurcation of NATO-led framework operations and US-led counter-terrorist operations was a doctrinal abomination to those seeking unified campaign effect. However, seen in its early stages, British involvement in Afghanistan was regarded as non-discretionary, proportional and appropriate, and it enjoyed broad-based political and popular support. The invasion of Iraq would change that.

If there is a single, defining error in Western grand strategy in the campaigns we have fought in Central and Western Asia since 2001, it is the Iraq invasion of 2003. Its perceived illegitimacy infected operations in Afghanistan in a way that even US President Barack Obama's more recent 'good war/dumb war' dichotomy would not fix; it created a profound strategic distraction for the US; it broke NATO Alliance unity; and it created a jihadist pretext. It also focused the residual US force elements in Afghanistan under national command on a counterterrorism campaign, which became increasingly distanced from NATO operations and ran the risk of compromising both.

This then provided the backdrop to the decision to commit British forces to the south of Afghanistan. After initial success, operations in Iraq became complex and protracted and in 2003–04 it was almost impossible to find a senior American willing to take Afghanistan seriously. Moreover, the increasing ferocity of the campaign against Al-Qa'ida in Iraq encouraged US national operations in Afghanistan to achieve comparable results, and what had been a distance between the NATO and US components of the campaign became mutually antithetical. By 2004–05 it began to look as if the NATO Alliance which had self-consciously re-defined itself beyond its original boundaries was about to fail in its first major expeditionary operation as member states shied away from further commitment without clear and unambiguous US leadership. It also began to look as if the unitary Afghan state was to be divided in half. In the north, the area broadly contiguous with the Uzbek, Tajik and Hazara elements of the Northern Alliance, constitutionally linked to Kabul, within which NATO forces operated with a light touch, and, with a strategic predilection for Indian support. In the south, a de facto Pashtunistan, with little more than a client relationship with Kabul, within which Taliban strength and cohesion was growing and US forces operated aggressively, underwritten by a strategic predilection for Pakistani support. This not only looked inimical to Afghan national unity, it also had the potential to define the start lines of the next round of regional conflict.

Above all, it was clear that if NATO failed then the UK strategic end would fail with it. The national strategic imperative therefore became the re-vivification of the Alliance campaign and its structural unification with discrete US operations. Clearly this was beyond British capability alone, but it was judged that the selective deployment of UK forces to the south of Afghanistan could act as a catalyst for the completion of the NATO plan and, crucially, to the decisive commitment of US forces that was the precondition to success.

The campaigns in Iraq and Afghanistan did not share a common strategic provenance, but they were unified to the extent that the UK only had one set of armed forces to prosecute them with. In turn, this implied choices about where those forces could be employed to greatest effect. The apparent, but illusory, success in the Multinational Division (South East) in 2003–04 encouraged the UK chiefs of staff to conclude that operations could be successfully maintained and concluded in Iraq, while, concurrently, a plan could be scoped in conjunction with close allies for the execution of the later phases of the NATO Afghan campaign.

The prior commitment of the UK HQ Allied Rapid Reaction Corps to command ISAF forces from May 2006 offered a target date for the Stage III deployment; it also offered the chance of British stewardship of a unified NATO-US operation. An Alliance force with the UK, Canada, the Netherlands and, somewhat reluctantly, the US at its core began to take shape and successive ISAF command tours by the Italians and British, extended to nine months each, were designed to give NATO forces a continuity of command that had not invariably characterised NATO operations in Afghanistan. The chiefs of staff were mindful that the south of Afghanistan was redolent with imperial legacy, as Kabul and Jalalabad had been previously, but this seemed a justifiable risk when taken alongside strategic failure. The Canadians established their tenure in Kandahar as a condition of entry, and, while Kandahar rather than Helmand would have been Britain's first choice, this was judged a necessary concession.

But at the heart of the unfolding deal was the guarantee of US forces to discharge the final stage of the overall plan and the unification of parallel command structures under a single NATO officer. This re-focusing of US attention back to the Afghan theatre coincided with the crisis of the Iraq campaign and the doctrinal re-definition of counter-insurgency operations, which would find full expression in the Iraq 'Surge'. The parlous state of the Iraq campaign provided sufficient stimulus for this to take place without consideration of its implications in Afghanistan. However, the unification of NATO and US national command structures represented a demonstrable emphasis upon counter-insurgency rather than counter-terrorism, and provided a minor chord to the overall debate in US doctrinal circles.

The deployment of NATO forces to the Stage III area of southwest Afghanistan began in early 2006 according to a tactical plan which deserves a separate record. Taken overall, the conduct of British operations in Central and Western Asia, 2001–15, will require a comprehensive audit of war at its completion. What can safely be said now is that the purpose of strategy is to provide the material link between government policy and results on the ground within the theatre of operations. That policy did not change and neither did its emphasis on a broad-based political outcome rather than something resembling a military victory; indeed, it was more vehemently advocated by the serving prime minister and others after 2006 than before.

Strategic choices between competing theatres is not a novel British dilemma, as students of the Westerners/Easterners debate, 1914–16, will recognise. What was novel about the choices made between the Afghan and Iraqi theatres was that they did not form part of a single conflict and the invasion of Iraq was driven by an external logic. The tensions that this created define the period from 2003 onwards, and represent the challenge to the historian of the period.

AFGHANISTAN AND THE CONTEXT OF IRAQ

NICK BEADLE

The Afghan deployment decisions of 2005 and 2006 benefit from being seen in the context of what else was happening at that time: this paper offers my view from the Private Office of the Ministry of Defence (MoD) from late summer 2005 to mid-2007 for defence secretaries John Reid and Des Browne. The UK was then mired in an unpopular war in Iraq, with declining consent at home; there were other tensions in the region, particularly in Pakistan; the US at that stage had not yet learnt its lessons of counter-insurgency; NATO was still divided; and Whitehall was run by a strongly Atlanticist, pragmatic but 'sofa government' and a disconnected Cabinet Office. The UK lacked a credible long-term strategy for the region, in which British interests were spelled out for departments of state. The Foreign Office was never able to answer the question of what our long-term interests and relative priorities were for Pakistan and Afghanistan, let alone how that meshed with our policy toward others in the region, including Iran and India.

Key questions were unanswered: Where was the grand strategy that previous Afghanistan campaigns had been fought on? What were the strategic objectives that could be honed into a convincing narrative worth fighting for? That was not for the military to define, and without a proper sense of what long-term influence we wanted in the region, we had little reference to measure our response. In 2005–06, I never found anything convincing on Afghanistan strategy from the international policy experts in Whitehall. In that vacuum, the NATO strategy – if a clock-face can be a strategy – ticked on as time does. Given the changing circumstances in Afghanistan and the region, and the declining support of partners, we failed to adequately challenge the basic NATO concept developed in 2002. It was very questionable how it could still be relevant following developments in Pakistan and at that stage the increasing US reluctance to a unified command – let alone the effect Iraq had on public consent. That was our moment to reset the agenda and that was our moment to reset the clock. We were as wrong about the timing of a new intervention as we were about the tactics and resources.

The 'Good' versus 'Bad' War

In the period leading up to the political agreement to the UK deployment to southern Afghanistan, there was a feeling in the Ministry of Defence that this was the 'military's war'. Aspiring and talented middle-ranking officers, particularly those that felt they had missed out on the early Iraq deployments, enthusiastically welcomed the idea of the Afghanistan deployment. In late 2005 they could sense Iraq operations had become unpopular with the British people and felt perhaps that it would reflect badly on them. John Reid was popular in the MoD Main Building not for his background as a previous minister for the armed forces, nor for his politics, but for delivering the military what they wanted. He was certainly not compliant; rather, he believed it was the right thing. Des Browne even more so. At the time, one very senior military officer was talking openly about how Afghanistan was the 'good war' and that we ought to be pushing to leave Iraq as soon as possible. Later, this dichotomy would become part of a public narrative that did much harm to the trust between military and government.

Of course, the 'get out of Iraq now' position was not universally shared. A number of military colleagues, for whom I have the utmost admiration, saw their wise counsel fail to change a momentum that defied the circumstances. Anything that went wrong in Iraq – and plenty did – fed the feeling we should not be there; whereas anything going right fed the idea we could draw down, and we did. Meanwhile, nothing outside the MoD seemed to trigger a challenge to the next phase of our commitment in Afghanistan. A new Afghan chapter was being written without a shot being fired.

Whitehall busied itself with Afghan narratives – I contributed to several. To see the policy, look to the contemporary speeches of politicians and military. There was not much grand strategy, but no shortage of the sentiment that 'something must be done' for Afghanistan. In hindsight, and to my shame, we had convinced ourselves of the need to go and go then. In the end, because we lacked the long-term strategic view for the region, the only outcome that we really offered to parliament and our people – an Afghan liberal democracy – was in fact what the country could not be. We announced a deployment subject to the action of our partners in order to force their hands. Making this caveat, and then seeing it matched (yet only in part), became the reason for going into Helmand.

Into Helmand

How then did we end up going to Helmand, rather than to Kandahar? I can offer nothing more as a reason than a failure to persuade the US to support us, as against the preference of the Canadians to go to Kandahar. The US rightly guessed we would go into southern Afghanistan anyway. Ministers were advised not to try to reverse decisions that had been made in military circles some time previously. The tail was wagging the dog: coalition military politics were driving national strategic interest. With hindsight, my impression is that diplomacy and politics followed rather tamely. Notable commanders, including General Richards, instinctively understood the strategic significance of Kandahar, with its links to Quetta in less-troubled times. If our long-term strategic priorities are in Pakistan and our security interests lie in the border regions, then we should have pushed harder to be at the centre of gravity of the region.

Nevertheless, we were set to deploy to Helmand during the early part of 2006. On 14 November 2005, John Reid made an important statement to the House of Commons:

> I will not announce the deployment to Helmand until I am satisfied that we have the military configuration that we ourselves need, and until we have the necessary back-up and resources across government here to provide alternative livelihoods to farmers whose current livelihood may be dependent on narcotics. To take away one form of income without substituting another would encourage insurgency rather than stability. Finally, I will not make that announcement until I believe that the multinational jigsaw has been put together and we have the necessary input from our NATO colleagues both in and around Helmand . . .

The chiefs of staff's un-minuted weekly briefings pored over the daily detail and longer-term deployment and logistics plans of Iraq, but with much less time being spent on Afghanistan. The ministerial briefings came at the end of chief of staff's weekly ones, and was an opportunity for all MoD ministers to raise issues. Some of the briefings were strategic; it was there that John Reid rehearsed his arguments. He sought reassurances to answer what he instinctively knew would be the foundation of a parliamentary scaffold. I was there when he said he would need, first, a credible NATO plan; second, commitments from other nations to adequately resource that plan; and third, a funded alternative livelihoods programme. Over the next few months he received those assurances. We went to Helmand thinking we had got it right, rather than hoping we had not got it wrong.

In the end, the national operational plan that was produced lacked credibility among the military, if only because they knew the weakest link of the chain was buying off the Afghans. There were no real alternative livelihoods we could deliver in short timeframes, and the belief that we would get good UK officials to go quickly into theatre and have properly funded projects was a triumph of optimism over experience. Arguably, as the NATO and UK plans underestimated the task, the coalition did not begin to deliver until 2009 what was required in Helmand in 2006.

In contrast, by mid-2005 Iraq was going through another iteration of the plan to dismantle the insurgency there. My second spell in Baghdad had been helping a small US team develop the 'Alternative Campaign Plan for Iraq'. This US plan urged a clear, hold and build policy based on the British counter-insurgency in Malaya of the 1950s. Central to the 'ink-spot' concept was the need to tackle the strategic population centres early on – Baghdad, Mosul and Basra. John Reid and Tony Blair understood the fresh approach to counter-insurgency, but were warned by officials that such a concept could not work in Afghanistan. The mantra that 'Afghanistan is not Iraq' was right in the generality, but, as a consequence, we were slower to learn things from each theatre. The 'Surge', as it was to become, took several months to emerge as a fully fleshed-out and properly resourced Washington initiative.

Why then did the UK and international effort in Afghanistan take so long to start delivering what was necessary? There has been speculation that it was a cap on resources that ruined a good plan. To an extent, the limit of resources will always impact on what can be done, but arriving at that limit is an iterative process. This is as true in a coalition sense as it is nationally. So knowing the limits is all part of the process of planning as well as a proper constraint of the military. Some of the more revisionist versions of what happened seek to convince us that the inadequacies of the plan were down to unrealistic resource limitations. This was not the whole case. Only once the plan was agreed were the limits imposed. Of course, there was a ceiling on the commitment in Afghanistan, but the numbers were understood and signed off by the military themselves. In Whitehall, it was No 10 and the Cabinet Office that fixed the ceiling, rather than the Treasury. In fact, the Treasury often complained that they were not included in discussions until too late.

Arguably, Whitehall knew a good deal more about the limitations of resource and rules of engagement than they did about the deployment itself. As a result, any plan for changes to our configuration, including the platoon houses in the Sangin valley, should have rung alarm bells, but did not. Ministers in the Ministry of Defence should have been better informed about what was happening on the ground. My own recollection is of a justification for the move based on it being a temporary deployment with an element of rescue attached. The fact there is any doubt about who knew what and when speaks volumes for the way in which this was briefed and handled at the Cabinet

Office level. Since 2004, the central Whitehall machinery has had a tendency to record history (in real-time) rather than direct it.

When Des Browne took over as defence minister in May 2006, the moment was marked by a tragic helicopter incident in Basra barely twenty-four hours into the job. It was a frantic ten days or so in what would be an exhausting six months. The perfect storm of a sharp increase in sectarian violence across Iraq following the Al-Askari Mosque bombing on the one hand, and the 'charge up the valley' in Helmand on the other, meant the circumstances had changed dramatically and we were not in a position to respond without seeking help from partners. Much has been made of Des Browne's newness in post, but I would argue strongly that during this period he was effective – questioning and probing to learn why things were done. He was well supported and while he did not bring nuanced defence policy to the debate in the early days, he knew the prime minister's intent and had good instincts.

Coalition Realities

As well as the issues around the structures and processes in Whitehall, there were also important shortcomings in the command structure in Afghanistan that contributed to the problems. Some of these were inherent to coalitions, others unique to Afghanistan.

Our ability to operate with partners and provide leadership of command where necessary is integral to the remarkable legacy of the British military. In both Iraq in 2003–05 and Afghanistan 2006–09, command at the level above the national task force commander was an issue. The co-ordination between Task Force Helmand, Regional Command South, and Kabul – at first confused by the twin commands of the US and NATO – seemed dislocated. The UK commanders on the ground appeared to have three masters: Permanent Joint Headquarters (PJHQ); MoD Main Building; and NATO. The extent to which the 'Chiefs' (not CDS) get into the operational detail can increase the perception of duplication between PJHQ and MoD Main Building. It is often waved away as a lack of understanding of the respective roles, but I have seen how the relationship with the task force commander can swing on the personalities of the Chief of Joint Operations at Northwood and (what was) DCDS(C) in Whitehall. The timing of changes of senior military leaders in a period of operations needs to be carefully judged. At the sector level in Afghanistan NATO has operational control, but there have been comments about how the was UK fighting its own war in its own way in a coalition environment.

At the political interface, NATO is often seen as a bureaucratic obstacle. Ministers have seen time and again the poor response of member states to force generation. It is a high price to pay for political legitimacy, while the imbalance of force provision is rarely a barrier to criticism from the non-contributing nations. In Afghanistan in 2006, there needed to be a better focus of NATO command. At the end of 2008, General Nick Carter provided that as the NATO commander in the south arriving with an explicit remit from General Stanley McChrystal to increase co-ordination and coherence. A new unifying NATO operational plan for the south based on a strategy that General Carter had been part of devising helped everyone. It was centred on creating areas of stability in the population-centric areas, starting with Kandahar and protecting routes in between. Also helpful was having a UK component commander in Kabul, General Nick Parker; but even with those two Britons in the command chain, there is no disguising the spat that ensued, with PJHQ demanding restrictions to prevent the dilution of control they exercised over the task-force commander. In a welcome move, the UK now provides for longer deployments for some senior officers, which have prompted better understanding of, and working relationships with, the US commanders in Afghanistan.

* * *

In conclusion, my perception is that across Whitehall there was a sense of redemption to be found in the proposed Afghanistan deployment and a drift toward denial about Iraq. If I do a disservice to friends and ex-colleagues, it is because I saw things through the prism of wanting to finish our operations in Iraq that would allow us to retain influence in the south of the country. We failed to deliver that legacy, largely because there was no long-term foreign policy plan, but also because the military hollowed out some force elements ahead of formal transition in order to feed the Afghan mission. As a response to the view that we took our eye off Afghanistan in 2003 because of Iraq, I would point out that we did the same in southern Iraq in 2006–07 because of our Afghan operations, with disastrous consequences. Our exit from Afghanistan must be better managed.

CONCLUSION

MICHAEL CLARKE

A former chief of the General Staff summed up the strategic issue around the Afghan campaign in a single question to which he himself had no satisfactory answer. 'How did we go', he asked, 'from the original intention to support the UN's ISAF mission in 2001 to the sombre spectacle of repatriating dead soldiers through Wootton Bassett ten years later?'[1] The question goes to the heart of how a political intention is arrived at and how it then finds expression, in this case largely through the military, to become 'policy'. The military establishment must necessarily be the servant of political direction. So did the original political intention in Afghanistan set a strategic course, after which all was merely tactical? Or were there missed opportunities to respond differently and to refine the original strategic intention to shape the flow of events and impose a better outcome to that which occurred by the end of 2006? These papers have sought to provide evidence to address this key strategic question.

Strategy and Political Intention

There is not much doubt about the genesis of the original political intention to engage in Afghanistan. The government was unambiguously committed from the outset. Prime Minister Tony Blair makes it clear in several passages of his memoir how clearly he saw it at the time. 'I was', he said of the evening of

[1] Author interview, 22 September 2011.

9/11, 'relatively calm, clear in my own mind what had to be done'.[2] More than President George W Bush, Tony Blair felt that he immediately appreciated the enormity of what happened on 11 September 2001 and that nothing would be quite the same again. There was, he said, 'no alternative path. It was war. It had to be fought and won . . . the madmen had declared war . . . the way we chose was to confront it militarily'.[3] He also felt that he had some sense, if not of the length of the task the West might be taking on in Afghanistan, at least of its deeper political implications. Fighting such a war, he says, 'requires nation-building. It requires a myriad of interventions deep into the affairs of other nations'.[4] His words represent an astonishing admission of certainty, even in ten years of retrospect. Alastair Campbell's diaries confirm exactly the same motivation from 9/11. He recorded late in the evening of that fateful day, 'the importance of the diplomatic strategy to support the United States . . . [and that it was] vital that we worked up an international agenda that went beyond the US just hitting Afghanistan'.[5] Other insiders at the time have offered similar interpretations of the instant mood, and there is no evidence that the fundamentals changed in the following weeks. When all US air space was closed in the hours after the attacks, the single aircraft that was given leave to fly into the US was one that left Britain carrying its intelligence chiefs for immediate consultations in the White House and with their US intelligence counterparts.

At the level of grand strategy, therefore, the political course was set from the beginning. The United Kingdom would support the United States to the hilt; the Taliban government in Afghanistan would be an immediate target of remedial or retaliatory action; and any conflict which ensued in

---

[2] Tony Blair, *A Journey* (London: Arrow Books, 2011), p. 351.

[3] *Ibid.*, pp. 345, 349. On the somewhat confused appreciation of George W Bush to the immediate events, see the account of one of his close staff, David Frum, *The Right Man: An Inside Account of the Surprise Presidency of George W Bush* (London: Weidenfeld and Nicolson, 2003), pp. 132–33.

[4] *Ibid.*, p. 349.

[5] Alastair Campbell, *The Alastair Campbell Diaries: Power and Responsibility, 1999–2001*, (London: Hutchinson, 2011), p. 694.

Afghanistan, it was correctly understood, would only be prelude to a broader campaign that would seek somehow to prevent that country again becoming hijacked by an international terrorist group such as Al-Qa'ida.

This grand strategy could have been fundamentally misconceived, of course. It is entirely plausible to argue that the better strategic response to the 9/11 attacks might have been to act in a more discriminating way, to treat the problem essentially as a matter of criminal justice rather than as a war, and not to assume that such problems are best confronted, in the manner of conventional security threats, as far away from the homeland as possible. Nevertheless, such an alternative approach was barely contemplated in Washington during the couple of years following the attacks.[6] Osama Bin Laden had explicitly declared war on America and the West in his celebrated fatwa of 1998 and this attack, more out of the blue than that of Pearl Harbor, generated a deep American anger that was easy to understand and difficult for allies not to share. For the British prime minister, the issue was immediate and uncomplicated. The Bush administration made it clear that the rest of the world could either be 'with us, or you are with the terrorists'.[7] It was time to take sides and it is barely conceivable that the UK would not stand, in Tony Blair's words, 'shoulder to shoulder' with the US in such circumstances.[8] No matter that Tony Blair's reaction was based almost entirely on instinct; he indicates that he would have supported a military response in Afghanistan with or without the history of the Anglo-American relationship at his back. In a crisis where US allies were called by Washington to stand up and be counted by their actions, he took a grand strategic decision that would have been entirely understood by Churchill, Macmillan, or Thatcher. In this respect, history might be kinder to him than his contemporaries have been.

If that was a comprehensible strategy, the next question, therefore, is how the rest of the system – in this case the higher

---

[6] See, for example, the evidence in John Kampfner, *Blair's Wars* (London: Simon and Schuster, 2003), pp. 152–73.

[7] Frum, *op. cit.*, p. 146.

[8] Blair, *op. cit.*, p. 341.

civil service and the military – sought to implement this political intention and influence its progress down the line in a way that was somehow consistent with a deeply understood set of intrinsic strategic objectives that serve British national interests; the extent, in other words, that the system showed evidence of a 'habit of strategic thinking' in a strategically literate manner.[9] Tony Blair's determination to stand 'shoulder to shoulder' with the United States could take many different forms and as a key military ally of Washington, the UK had a number of opportunities to influence US policy, some of which it clearly tried to use.[10]

A convincing case is made in this volume by Rob Fry and Desmond Bowen that if the international focus had remained on Afghanistan, and not so heavily refocused on Iraq after mid-2002, the course of events in Afghanistan might have been different. There is no serious dispute that the years from 2001 to 2006 saw little to make good on the assertion that the US and its allies would not 'turn their backs' on Afghanistan once the Taliban had been chased off; these were essentially wasted years for the Afghans. This was evident to insider opinion, certainly by 2003. So for the UK, the 'sub-strategic question' of continuing to give effect to the prime minister's intention increasingly appeared to revolve around a choice either to stand by while the Afghan part of the whole policy failed after 2003–04, or to re-engage with the original commitment to give it some chance of ultimate success.

Why the UK, of all countries, should take on this galvanising role in Afghanistan if the US could not, or would not, goes to the heart of the way the system works to give effect to political direction on defence and security questions, especially where the United States is concerned. It arose because a consensus in the policy machinery regarded it as axiomatic that the UK should seek to play a strategically significant role in US policy; not just to make a useful contribution, but to be a consequential ally – one that could

---

[9] The wording refers to the celebrated call of then-Chief of the Defence Staff, Jock Stirrup, at RUSI, London, 3 December 2009, calling for 'the habit of thinking strategically' among British defence professionals. Available at < http://www.rusi.org/events/past/ref:E4B184DB05C4E3/>.

[10] Kampfner, *op. cit.*, pp. 174–93.

make things happen in the world. This, it could be argued, was a powerful instinct that ran consistently through most of the policy machine; it was one of the particular 'habits of strategic thinking' that was hard to break, and was certainly strong among the military, which played a big role in giving effect to Tony Blair's original intentions. The UK was not just one of Washington's good allies; it could act as a strategically significant ally in its own right.

Command and Coherence

If it was to play a significant role, however, these papers also offer evidence of some critical inadequacies in the way the politico-military system operated in this particular case. They all bear heavily on the way the UK conducted operations in a complex and multinational context; conditions that are ubiquitous in contemporary conflicts. They suggest lessons which will apply to almost all operations in the foreseeable future.

As one part of a big multinational effort, a clear inadequacy in this operation was over-complexity both in the multinational, and even in the national, command chains. The UK was taking the lead in what had become an alliance operation, and was commanding NATO's Allied Rapid Reaction Corps (ARRC) which became the headquarters of ISAF in Kabul, under UK command led by General David Richards. But British forces deployed to Helmand as Task Force Helmand were originally included in the US-led counter-terrorist Operation *Enduring Freedom* which, in Regional Command (South), came under the control of a Canadian brigadier, David Frazer. But Task Force Helmand was also under national command, reporting directly to the Permanent Joint Headquarters (PJHQ) at Northwood. The command chain, therefore, encompassed ISAF, which was designed to operate both military and civil assets throughout the country and to partner the Afghans in the task of governance; Operation *Enduring Freedom*, led in Kandahar by Brigadier David Frazer, and with whom relations were not close; NATO, which was providing the authority for most of the European forces to be deployed in coalition; and the national command chain that went back directly to Northwood.

This was clearly an unsatisfactory arrangement that had been hastily agreed, partly on the basis that in a non-combat situation it could all be worked out in slower time as events progressed. But in the combat situation that actually developed so quickly, the command chain became a critical element. Within a few months it was streamlined. The incoming chief of the Defence Staff in London worked hard to get the Kandahar command upgraded to a two-star position to give it more coherence in controlling operations in the south, and at the end of July, David Richards, the ISAF commander, took over all operations in the country and folded Operation *Enduring Freedom* into ISAF operations. For the most critical months that set the course of the campaign, however, from February through July, the original lines of command – 'about as clear and neat as twigs in a bird's nest' – were a severe handicap to coherent strategic behaviour.[11]

It was no accident that Brigadier Ed Butler found himself operating from an itinerant command post that constantly moved between Kabul, Kandahar, Camp Bastion, and Lashkar Gah; caught between his senior commanders in Kabul and Kandahar and his subordinate commanders in Lashkar Gah, where his deputy was based, and Camp Bastion, where his main force was gathered.[12] Not least, all of this was supposed to mesh with a multinational aid and development effort, where the deployed civilians were intended to be intrinsic to operations, but where their personnel numbers were dwarfed by those of the military.[13]

The importance of such over-complexity is that it makes the expression of good 'strategic literacy' throughout the force very

[11] Stephen Grey, *Operation Snakebite: The Explosive True Story of an Afghan Desert Siege* (London: Viking Press, 2009), p. 51.

[12] Butler's deputy, Colonel Charlie Knaggs, was based with the British Provincial Reconstruction Team that had been operating for some time in Lashkar Gah. Butler was forced to command his force largely through intensive liaison with Colonel Knaggs. This might have been a reasonable arrangement if the operation had remained focused on aid and development. But in the context of combat, it was a further hindrance to efficient command and control.

[13] James Fergusson, *A Million Bullets: The Real Story of the British Army in Afghanistan* (London: Corgi Books, 2009), pp. 201–06.

difficult to achieve. It runs counter to the military culture of allowing a commander to make his intentions well-understood and to have a chain of command that uses initiative and invention to work towards a common purpose. Above all, it creates a machine that devours time and effort spent in co-ordination; it has an unquenchable appetite for liaison. But co-ordination is not strategy, or even strategic literacy. Co-ordination and liaison may pass for a sort of strategy because they establish what all parties agree upon. But in a multinational, civil-military operation, this can, at best, be regarded as a 'business strategy' approach to achieving objectives, rather than a serious security strategy.

In Afghanistan, actual combat exposed all these weaknesses. There was a general problem in understanding the necessary relationship between the 'ends', 'ways' and 'means' to do the job and getting broad-based political support for it. The task and the necessary resources were never properly matched at the most critical early stages. This was not only down to the limitations on the size of the initial force set by the politicians, or even the Treasury; the military and the Ministry of Defence (MoD) share some of the responsibility for failing to assess the 'ways and means' that might be required if the operation did not go well from the outset. The byzantine multinational command structure contributed to the momentum that made a deployment, even a mal-deployment, unstoppable.

More particularly, the early command arrangements affected the single most important military decision at that stage of the campaign. When it came to moving north into platoon houses at the end of May 2006, the complex liaison machinery ensured that no one of significance could realistically claim they knew nothing about the move. Ministers, officials, military chiefs and civilian organisers all knew what was being proposed. But that does not, in itself, demonstrate that the strategic implications of what was going to happen were grasped by those in the system who would have to take responsibility for the outcome. Almost the opposite appears to have been the case. In British military culture, the man on the ground tends to be given great discretion to make key operational decisions. But the man on the ground, Brigadier Butler, had felt from the planning stages that the operation was not realistically resourced and that he now had few options but to go into a combat mode rather than adopt a classic counter-insurgency posture. Arguments continue over whether that was inevitably forced upon him by the circumstances, or whether he and his subordinate commanders made a tactical mistake which had strategic consequences. But none of the key commanders – Brigadier Butler and Colonels Charlie Knaggs and Stuart Tootal below him, or the ISAF commander, General David Richards – were well served by the web of command chains that surrounded the operation during this period.

The PJHQ was Brigadier Butler's main contact in his national command chain; but it does not operate as a military strategic headquarters. It does not interface with key political decision-makers as a matter of course. That interaction takes place at the MoD in London where ministers are briefed by the chiefs of staff, who are themselves kept fully informed on a regular basis, but are not central to operational decision-making. So those military officers talking regularly to the most relevant ministers – in London at the MoD – were not the ones making the decisions; the military officers who were making the decisions – in Afghanistan and at PJHQ in Northwood – talked mainly to each other. This resulted in a situation of intensive co-ordination with information being shared and discussed extensively throughout the system, but not necessarily in a way that aided understanding or helped in the identification of those decision points that were likely to have strategic consequences.

Such over-complexity in the command arrangement points to a second, related, problem in running a 'comprehensive approach' in the theatre of operations that attempts to bring all the various instruments of policy into line. As the paper by Valentina Soria demonstrates, the aspiration to be 'comprehensive' makes even greater demands on the system to be strategically literate in all sectors and at all levels. It involves extensive liaison between 'stakeholders' on a continuing basis, creating another mechanism that absorbs time and effort, but which may also serve to confuse the strategic importance of what is taking place on the ground. The efforts which went into horizontal co-ordination both in Whitehall and Afghanistan were considerable. Whitehall insiders frankly admit, however, that well co-ordinated policy is no substitute for a properly integrated policy. As one officer characterised it, the Whitehall machinery is like a series of independently spinning wheels. Sometimes their revolutions coincide to produce a very efficient drive mechanism, but there is no natural gearing mechanism in the system of sufficient force to ensure that this happens when politicians want it to. Co-ordinating the different speeds and arcs in which they spin is not the same as harnessing their collective energy to drive the engine of policy implementation. It is hardly surprising that the 'comprehensive approach' in Whitehall has effectively been replaced by an attempt to create an 'integrated approach' that extends principally to the MoD, Foreign Office and DfID. If these three ministries can arrive at a single policy objective that is genuinely agreed, and also meaningful, then other relevant ministries and agencies can base their plans on that central core.

In the case of Afghanistan, however, even this more modest objective was effectively beyond the UK's reach. Whatever the UK did, and however well co-ordinated its response, the UK's achievement of some parts of the 'comprehensive approach' was no more than a small part of the whole multinational military-civil effort and, as such, a tiny part of the effort required to build a viable state in Afghanistan over a number of years. If this lesson has been well-learned in the years since 2006, it remains astonishing that such cavalier optimism should have prevailed at the outset of the operation; so little account being taken of the vast and complex development challenges that Afghanistan posed.

Most of all, the Afghan decisions of 2005–06, when Iraq had become unexpectedly testing, demonstrate how difficult it has become for UK strategy to deal with two big things at once. The paper by Nick Beadle shows just how difficult it was for the system as a whole, rather than the individuals in it, to join up all the dots on the Afghan strategy when Iraq dominated every significant planning conversation. At a tactical level, the military can deal with two operational theatres simultaneously; it is a straightforward matter of managing limited resources between two separate purposes. But it is not clear that the system is also able to take in its stride the political/military interface at the right level and to identify the key moments; recognising when those moments arrive and being able to take big decisions, such as committing significantly more resources, or being prepared to limit or halt a deployment.

The Military in Policy-making

Accusations have been made, both general and specific, that the British military drove the UK's policy on Afghanistan to an unacceptable degree, since it wanted to engage in a 'redemptive' operation in Afghanistan after the moral ambiguity of the Iraq War. And more serious allegations were the subject of a public argument between General Richard Dannatt, a former chief of the General Staff, and Sherard Cowper-Coles, a former ambassador in Kabul, who claimed that the army was looking for a role in Afghanistan, specifically to avoid a 'use them or lose them' choice after the drawdown of troops from Northern Ireland.[14] Writers such as Frank Ledwidge, Rory Stewart and Patrick Little have argued that the problems surrounding the Afghan deployment have been conventionally blamed on the politicians and the Treasury, but equally reflect deep failures of thinking and strategy within the military itself, and particularly within the army.[15]

These papers are concerned only with the origins of the Helmand deployment rather than the whole campaign, but they provide support for a number of propositions. One is that the military had an important role in creating the original momentum to re-engage with the Afghan policy in 2003 and hitching the UK to that particular policy engine. The paper by Matthew Willis details how far the discussions between military officials in Washington,

---

[14] House of Commons Foreign Affairs Committee, *The UK's Foreign Policy Approach to Afghanistan and Pakistan*, HC 514 (London, The Stationery Office, March 2011); see also *Guardian*, 'Afghan Envoy Apologised over Troop Redeployment Claims, says Dannatt', 20 January 2011.

[15] Frank Ledwidge, *Losing Small Wars: British Military Failure in Iraq and Afghanistan* (New Haven, CT: Yale University Press, 2011); Rory Stewart, *Occupational Hazards: My Time Governing in Iraq* (London: Picador, 2007); Patrick Little, 'Lessons Unlearned: A Former Officer's Perspective on the British Army', *RUSI Journal* (Vol. 154, No. 3, June 2009).

Ottawa, London and The Hague created a particular framework for action that was then endorsed at the political level in NATO, after which it became unstoppable alliance policy. It might be tweaked and adjusted, but the momentum of re-engagement appears to have emerged from a military liaison process, rather than to have been an initiative coming out of a Cabinet meeting in London. Interviews have also indicated that as that process moved along, British military officers were given assurances by their American counterparts that US forces would be backing up the deployment. But there is certainly no recollection of such a firm commitment among UK government officials or diplomats and it was never committed to paper. It appears that US assurances were 'over-interpreted' by British military officers and then accepted within the policy process in London.[16]

This gives some credence to a more general criticism articulated by Sherard Cowper-Coles that the British Army suffers from a natural 'conspiracy of optimism' in contemplating operations and that the general expertise of the military tends to overawe the judgements of civil servants and even diplomats.[17] The reality, however, cannot be quite so glibly expressed. At senior levels in the army itself, there was certainly something that alternated between optimism and a determination to cope with the demands being made on it. The army's commander-in-chief in the lead-up to the deployment during 2005 was Richard Dannatt and his account expresses exactly the mixture of a 'can do' approach alongside a sense of duty to try to square some very demanding circles.[18] Lower down the chain, however, the commanders of Task Force Helmand were much less optimistic. The same 'can do' attitude applied but in a different way. Brigadier Butler felt compelled into a combat role for which they were not well-equipped, while some observers – and other military officials in London – have accused the commanders of the 3 Para battlegroup of 'spoiling

---

[16] Author interview, 13 October 2011.

[17] Sherard Cowper-Coles, *Cables from Kabul: The Inside Story of the West's Afghanistan Campaign* (London: Harper Collins, 2011), pp. 280–81.

[18] Richard Dannatt, *Leading From the Front* (London: Bantam Press, 2010), pp. 224, 235–37.

for a fight' once they arrived in theatre, and being glad enough to be compelled into combat operations.[19] Other military professionals, both retired and serving, were gravely concerned at what the army was taking on with the resources of a single battlegroup.[20] Whatever the rights and wrongs of these perceptions, it is evident that there was little strategic coherence from top to bottom of the politico-military system during the early stages of the deployment.

Equally, the accusation that the military were naturally dominant in policy discussions with civilian officials must be set in the context of the wider circumstances. The permanent undersecretary in the Ministry of Defence in 2005, Sir Kevin Tebbit, told the Chilcot Inquiry that he had serious concerns about the coming deployments to Helmand, but did not voice them strongly enough at the time.[21] This was hardly the result of timidity on his part, but rather the sheer distraction of operations in Iraq and the demands they were making on his ministry, about which he had a great deal to say. The problem seems to have been more that the British military was part of a multinational military structure, preparing to deploy as part of Britain's most important alliance – NATO – and for the sake largely of Britain's most important partner, the United States. British military policy-makers felt as constrained as everyone else in the system by the press of events, and if they were not being robustly challenged by those who had doubts about the operation, it seems to have been because few officials could see any better alternative than to press on.

However we eventually interpret the outcome of Britain's fourth Afghan War – very different, to be sure, from the previous three – the process of engagement in it during 2006 was less than

---

[19] Ledwidge, *op. cit.*, pp. 72, 79.

[20] Some retired military chiefs now in the House of Lords have revealed that they spoke strongly and privately against the deployment in the way it was being contemplated, but that their opinions were discounted.

[21] Transcript of oral evidence given by Sir Kevin Tebbit to the Chilcot Inquiry, 3 February 2010, pp. 14–17, available at <http://www.iraqinquiry.org.uk/transcripts/oralevidence-bydate/100203.aspx>, accessed 2 December 2011.

satisfactory from almost every point of view.[22] The question remains whether this was down to a failure of international strategy, of which the UK was a part; a failure of UK strategy, that implicated other allies; or a half-decent strategy that has taken some time to achieve momentum within Afghanistan itself. All these interpretations are plausible from the available evidence, and a satisfactory answer is not likely for some years to come. Nevertheless, it is painfully evident how little strategic literacy there was in the UK's decision-making system during the critical years from 2001 to 2006. Individuals had their own views and acted from the best of intentions. But the system as a whole seemed to have had no strategic brain; no self-awareness of the full scale of the potential challenge, or a settled procedure for taking new challenges in its stride. After a decade of engagement in a troubled country, this is a sombre reflection on British strategic thinking.

[22] It should be noted that Britain created a precarious stalemate in the first Afghan War of 1839–42, and unambiguously won the next two wars, in 1878–80 and 1919. Throughout this long period the essential strategic aim of these conflicts – to keep Russian influence away from British India – was largely achieved.

About Whitehall Papers

The *Whitehall Paper* series provides in-depth studies of specific developments, issues or themes in the field of national and international defence and security. Published occasionally throughout the year, *Whitehall Papers* reflect the highest standards of original research and analysis, and are invaluable background material for specialists and policy-makers alike.

About RUSI

The Royal United Services Institute (RUSI) is an independent think tank engaged in cutting-edge defence and security research. A unique institution, founded in 1831 by the Duke of Wellington, RUSI embodies nearly two centuries of forward thinking, free discussion and careful reflection on defence and security matters.

RUSI consistently brings to the fore vital policy issues to both domestic and global audiences, enhancing its growing reputation as a 'thought-leader institute', winning the Prospect Magazine Think Tank of the Year Award 2008 and Foreign Policy Think Tank of the Year Award 2009 and 2011. RUSI is a British institution, but operates with an international perspective. Satellite offices in Doha and Washington, DC reinforce its global reach. It has amassed over the years an outstanding reputation for quality and objectivity. Its heritage and location at the heart of Whitehall, together with a range of contacts both inside and outside government, give RUSI a unique insight and authority.